VOLUME TWO
Japanese Army Bombers, Transports & Miscellaneous Types
New Guinea & the Solomons 1942-1944

MICHAEL JOHN CLARINGBOULD

Avonmore Books

Pacific Profiles Volume Two
Japanese Army Bombers, Transports & Miscellaneous Types
New Guinea & the Solomons 1942-1944

Michael John Claringbould
ISBN: 978-0-6486659-9-1

First published 2020 by Avonmore Books
Avonmore Books
PO Box 217
Kent Town
South Australia 5071
Australia

Phone: (61 8) 8431 9780
www.avonmorebooks.com.au

 A catalogue record for this book is available from the National Library of Australia

Cover design & layout by Diane Bricknell

© 2020 Avonmore Books.
No part of this book may be reproduced or transmitted in any form or by any means, electronic or mechanical, including photocopying or recording, or by any information storage and retrieval system, without permission in writing from the publisher.

Cover artwork captions

Front: A panoply of colour showcases the variety of JAAF markings in New Guinea. Top to bottom are a 10th Sentai Ki-46 Dinah, 7th Sentai Ki-49 Helen, 6th Hikoshidan Ki-21 Sally, 26th Sentai Ki-51 Sonia and a 75th Sentai Ki-48 Lily.

Rear: A 26th Sentai Ki-51 Sonia wanders the hinterlands of Wewak, surveying and photographing locations for river crossings. This type was often confused by Allied pilots as either a Zero or Oscar.

Contents

About the Author 5

Introduction 6

Chapter 1 – JAAF Bombers and Support Types in the South Pacific 13

Chapter 2 – Technical Notes 16

Chapter 3 – The 7th *Hiko Sentai* 21

Chapter 4 – The 14th *Hiko Sentai* 29

Chapter 5 – The 26th *Hiko Sentai* 37

Chapter 6 – The 34th *Hiko Sentai* 43

Chapter 7 – The 45th *Hiko Sentai* 49

Chapter 8 – The 60th *Hiko Sentai* 57

Chapter 9 – The 61st *Hiko Sentai* 61

Chapter 10 – The 75th *Hiko Sentai* 65

Chapter 11 – The 208th *Hiko Sentai* 69

Chapter 12 – Headquarters and Command Units 75

Chapter 13 – Reconnaissance Units 83

Chapter 14 – Transport and Liaison Units 95

Sources 110

Index of Names 112

The author with friends in the Papua New Guinea highlands, 2017.

About the Author

Michael Claringbould – Author & Illustrator

Michael spent his formative years in Papua New Guinea in the 1960s, during which he became fascinated by the many WWII aircraft wrecks which still lie around the country. Michael has served widely overseas as an Australian diplomat, including in South East Asia and throughout the South Pacific where he had the fortune to return to Papua New Guinea for three years commencing in 2003.

Michael has authored and illustrated various books on Pacific War aviation. His history of the Tainan Naval Air Group in New Guinea, *Eagles of the Southern Sky*, received worldwide acclaim as the first English-language history of a Japanese fighter unit, and was translated into Japanese. An executive member of Pacific Air War History Associates, Michael holds a pilot license and PG4 paraglider rating. He continues to develop his skills as a digital 3D aviation artist, using 3DS MAX, Vray and Photoshop to attain markings accuracy.

Other Books by the Author

Black Sunday (2000)

Eagles of the Southern Skies (2012, with Luca Ruffato)

South Pacific Air War Volume 1: The Fall of Rabaul December 1941–March 1942 (2017, with Peter Ingman)

P-39 / P-400 Airacobra versus A6M2/3 Zero-sen New Guinea 1942 (Osprey, 2018)

South Pacific Air War Volume 2: The Struggle for Moresby March–April 1942 (2018, with Peter Ingman)

Pacific Adversaries Volume One Japanese Army Air Force vs The Allies New Guinea 1942-1944 (2019)

South Pacific Air War Volume 3: Coral Sea & Aftermath May-June 1942 (2019, with Peter Ingman)

P-47D Thunderbolt versus Ki-43 Hayabusa New Guinea 1943/44 (Osprey, 2020)

Pacific Adversaries Volume Two Imperial Japanese Navy vs The Allies New Guinea & the Solomons 1942-1944 (2020)

Operation I-Go Yamamoto's Last Offensive – New Guinea and the Solomons April 1943 (2020)

Pacific Profiles Volume One Japanese Army Fighters New Guinea & the Solomons 1942-1944 (2020)

Pacific Adversaries Volume Three Imperial Japanese Navy vs The Allies New Guinea & the Solomons 1942-1944 (2020)

South Pacific Air War Volume 4: Buna & Milne Bay June – September 1942 (2020, with Peter Ingman)

Pacific Profiles Volume Three – Allied Medium Bombers, A20 Series, South West Pacific 1942-1944 (2021)

Introduction

This second volume of the *Pacific Profiles* series has the objective of portraying, as accurately as possible, the colours and unit markings of Japanese Army Air Force bombers and support types in the New Guinea theatre from 1942 to 1944. This objective is ambitious. As explained in *Pacific Profiles Volume One*, identifying JAAF unit markings in many cases can be a dark and hazardous art. Despite official yet ambiguous guidelines, such markings remained the prerogative of individual units, and as such largely lay within that narrow domain where they stayed. The colours and camouflage schemes provoked by this hostile theatre arguably produced the most diverse, yet haphazard, patterns in any air force of the Second World War. This created circumstances whereby markings of unrelated units could and were often similar. No official co-ordinated or centralised databases were compiled for JAAF unit markings.

However, this commonality is shared to some extent with the markings of its American counterpart in New Guinea – the USAAF Fifth Air Force. While certain theatre markings such as white wing leading edges and tails applied to single-engine fighters were officially decreed, the colourful heraldry systems and nose-art applied within squadrons were not. Most USAAF fighters in the theatre also had unique "buzz" or squadron numbers applied, and many of the bomber units applied unique alphabetic letters. No co-ordinated official lists for these exist either.

A paucity of adequate reference material has impeded past attempts to properly catalogue JAAF markings, especially the plethora of bomber, reconnaissance, transport, command, maintenance, air photo and liaison units in the wide theatre. Imaginative extrapolation and colour-guessing has created and sometimes consolidated false myths still perpetrated to this day, including markings which did not, in fact, exist. Often colours have been decided from monochrome images, a tempting but imperfect occupation.

Four decades of collecting material on this arcane subject has proved rewarding. Few publications, including Japanese-language ones, agree on interpretations, colours or even unit assignments. New Guinea, it seems, remains a lost theatre for the JAAF. The complexity of JAAF bomber and support operations in this challenging realm saw them operate alongside an eclectic inventory of fighters, covered in detail in *Pacific Profiles Volume One*.

Overpowering Allied technology and numbers eventually expelled the Imperial Japanese Army's 4th Air Force from the theatre. Thousands died in a jungle retreat. An inflexible Tokyo high command, far removed from the daily low-level terrors of Allied bombings, nonetheless ordered some units to withdraw their aircraft from Hollandia to Manila just in time.

INTRODUCTION

The colours and camouflage schemes provoked by this hostile theatre arguably produced the most diverse, yet haphazard, patterns in any air force of the Second World War. Some units, such as the 208th *Sentai*, chose to remove their tail heraldry in favour of more practical camouflage.

There were two types of markings which were ubiquitous across all types. A white combat band around the rear fuselage was applied to all JAAF airframes serving in combat zones. Described in *kanji* as the *"gaisei butai shikitai"*, this long-winded formal phrase translates essentially as the "Overseas Campaign Band". Around mid-1942 it became general practice for propellers and spinners to be wholly painted in "red bean" with a satin finish. Propeller tips were changed from red to yellow and data squares were stencilled to each blade near the hub. In some units, spinners were painted in distinguishing *chutai* or even *shotai* colours, either the whole spinner of just the forward half, or even a narrow band in between. This practice was more common in fighter units, however.

On 27 June 1945, Flight Lieutenant L Green, an Air Technical Intelligence Unit inspector, forwarded a report to RAAF Command in Brisbane on the results of his survey trip to Wewak and surrounds. This was to specifically reconnoitre wrecked Japanese aircraft abandoned at the airfields of But, Dagua, Wewak and Boram. The collection of aircraft destroyed and abandoned was staggering and included: 21 x Ki-51s, one Tachikawa Ki-55 trainer, one Mansyu Ki-79 Advanced Trainer, 51 x Ki-46 Dinahs, 59 x Ki-48 *Sokei* light bombers, 28 x Ki-49 *Donryu* heavy bombers and three Ki-57 transports. After adding the fighters present the total wreck inventory was 480. Despite the indifferent reaction from his masters in Melbourne, Green was not to know how invaluable reports like his would become in later years to historians, alongside similar tomes of documentation.

I hope you enjoy understanding the colours and markings rationale of these mercurial Japanese incumbents which briefly appeared in New Guinea skies so many years ago.

Michael John Claringbould
Canberra, Australia
July 2020

Technical Note
All profiles and other artwork in this volume were created from 3D models built in Autodesk 3DS MAX and rendered with Vray. Post-production work was completed with Photoshop.

Pacific Profiles Glossary

Japanese terms are in italics. All Japanese names are presented in the traditional way of writing Japanese, with the surname presented first.

ATIU	Air Technical Intelligence Unit
Chutai	An aircraft formation which normally comprised a strength of nine aircraft. JAAF bomber units normally had three *chutai*, Nos. 1, 2 and 3, plus a headquarters detachment.
Chutaicho	A flight leader of officer rank who commands a JAAF *chutai*.
CO	Commanding Officer
Dokuritsu Chutai	Independent *chutai* (or Independent Squadrons), often reconnaissance units, which reported directly to their parent *Hikodan*.
Dokuritsu Hikotai	An Independent unit similar to but larger than a *Dokuritsu Chutai*, although not so large as to be divided into *chutai*. These units were part of the JAAF's pre-Pacific War structure.
Donryu	Storm Dragon (JAAF name for Ki-49 "Helen" bomber)
Hayabusa	Peregrine Falcon (JAAF name for Ki-43 "Oscar" fighter)
Hei	aircraft variant, third model
Hentai	The pre-WWII definition originally meant a flight of three aircraft; however the *hentai* was a more structured unit with an administrative function built in. In WWII the term was applied to small groups of aircraft with their own built-in command and administrative structures which could be moved or transferred at short notice. Command and transport units sometimes had *hentai*.
Hien	Flying Swallow (JAAF name for Ki-61 "Tony" fighter)
Hiko Sentai	A JAAF Flying Regiment, often abbreviated to *sentai*.
Hikodan	A JAAF Flying Brigade which comprised two or more *Hiko Sentai*.
Hikoshidan	A JAAF Flying Division which comprised two or more *Hikodan*.
Hinomaru	The red disc on the Japanese flag representing the sun and also used as a roundel on Japanese aircraft.
Hiragana	Japanese phonetic lettering system.
Hiryu	Flying Dragon (official name for the Ki-67 "Peggy" bomber)
Hokoku	Inscriptions (translating as "patriotic") which signified that an aircraft was donated by an individual, organisation or corporation. The donor's name appeared in the *kanji* subscript. Note: in practice the JAAF preferred the term *aikoku* which had an identical meaning.
HQ	Headquarters
IJA	Imperial Japanese Army
IJN	Imperial Japanese Navy

JAAF	Japanese Army Air Force
Kanji	Adopted Chinese characters used as part of Japanese writing. In the case of the IJN, they were used alongside *katakana*. IJN wartime script uses many characters no longer recognisable in modern Japanese. All Japanese crew lists had their names written in *kanji*.
Katakana	Phonetic characters used in written Japanese, usually used for geographic place names.
Kitai	Numbers assigned to different aircraft types, issued by the JAAF chronologically regardless of type.
Ko	aircraft variant, first model
Kokugun	Air Force
Kumogata	Cloud-style camouflage pattern
MN	Manufacturer's Number
NEI	Netherlands East Indies
Otsu	aircraft variant, second model
Sakura	Cherry blossom symbol
Sentai	Abbreviation of *hiko sentai* defining a JAAF flying regiment.
Shotai	A Japanese term defining a JAAF flight, usually of three aircraft. However, in New Guinea such flights could also comprise two or four aircraft.
Shotaicho	Flight leader of a shotai
Sokei	A colloquial Japanese abbreviation of *shiki-souhatu-keibaku* often used to refer to the Ki-48 "Lily" light bomber.
USAAF	United States Army Air Force
VIP	Very Important Person
Yuso Hikotai	Independent Transport Flight

PACIFIC PROFILES

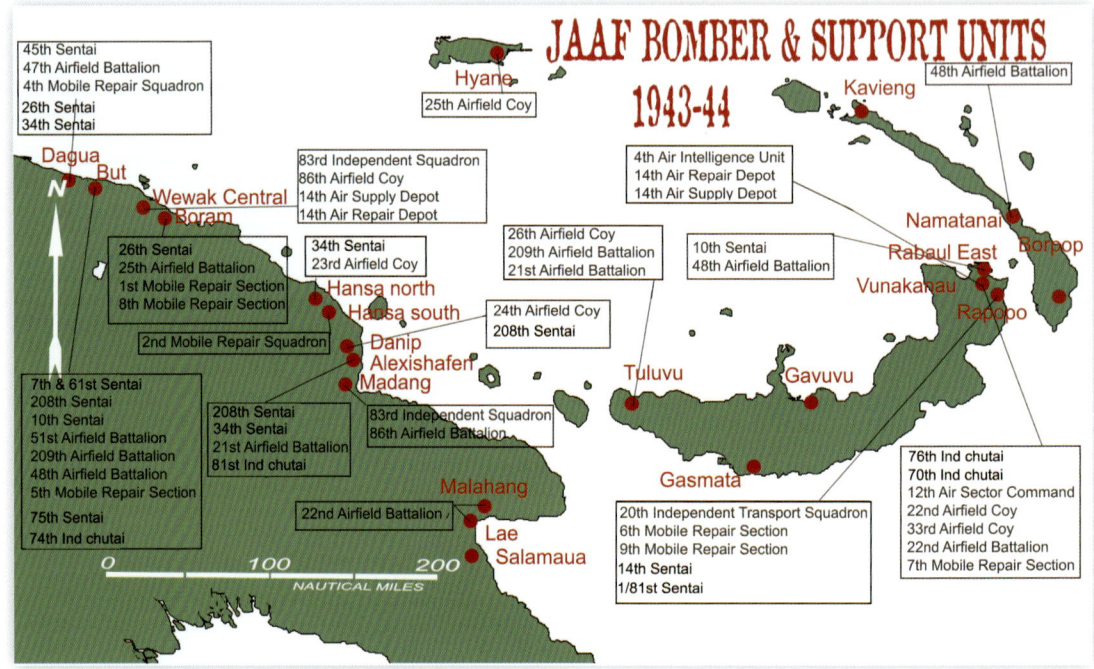

A map showing the locations of JAAF bomber and support units throughout New Guinea in 1943-44.

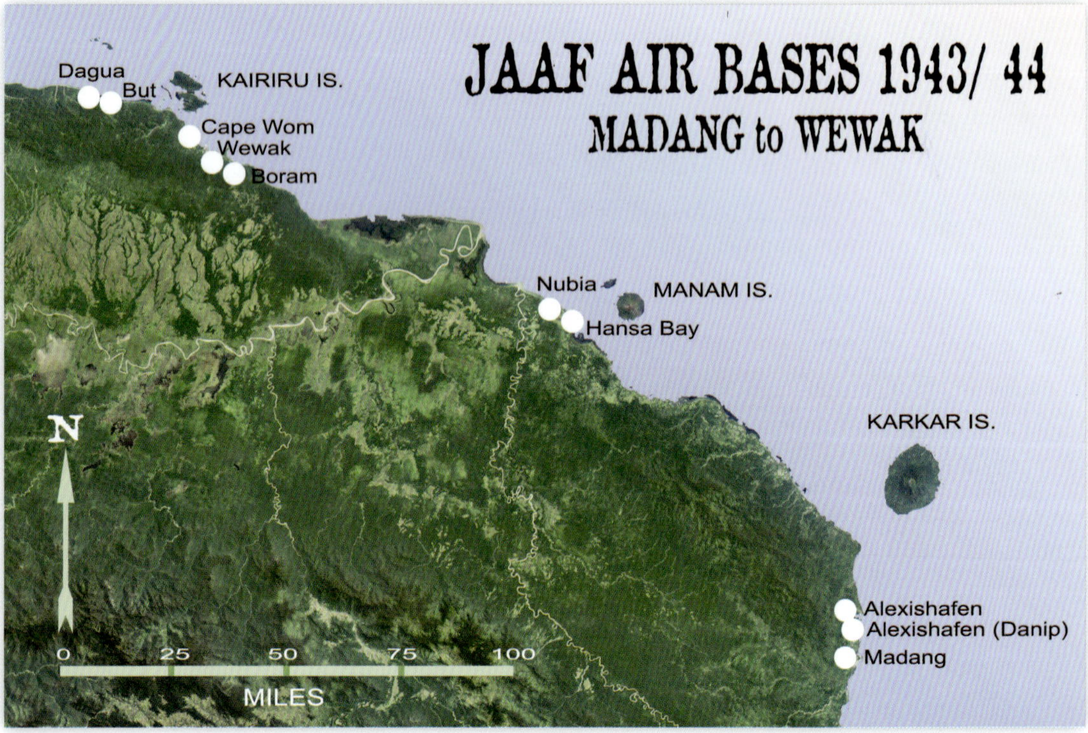

The location of JAAF air bases along the northern New Guinea coast between Madang and Wewak. This area was the stronghold of JAAF operations during 1943-44.

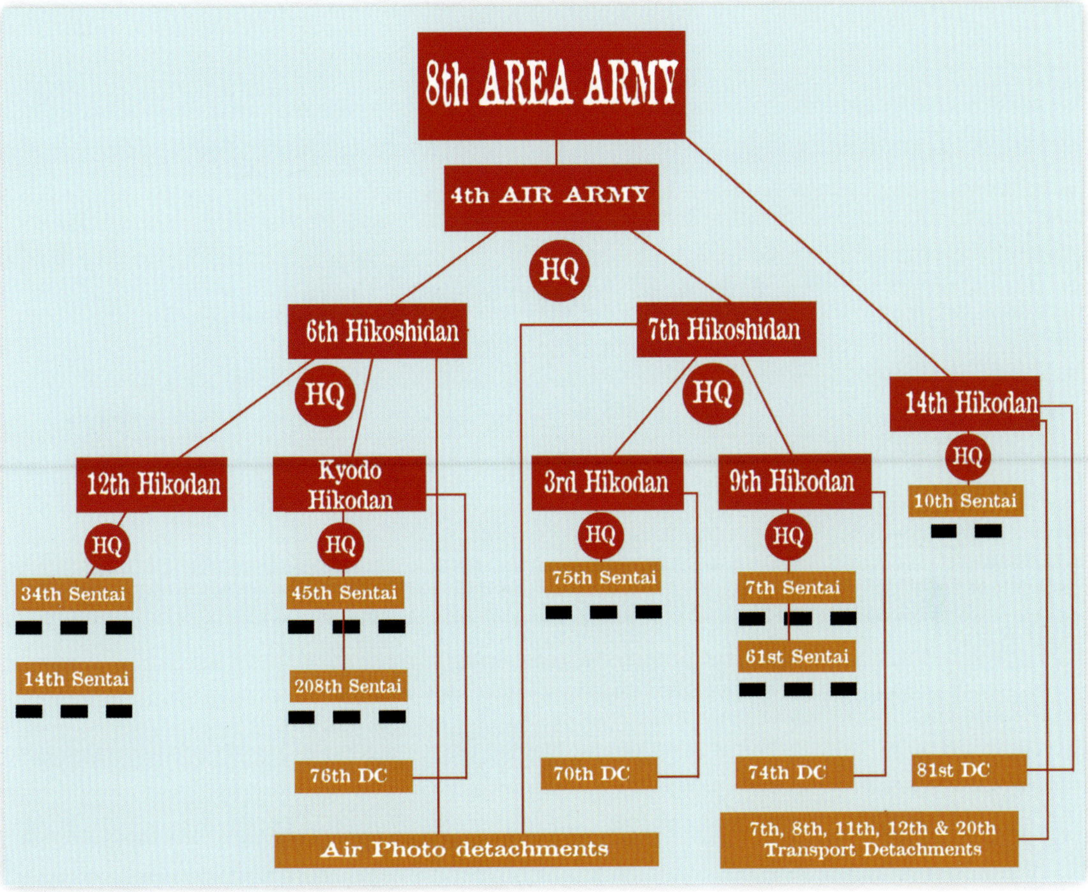

PACIFIC PROFILES

The organisational structure of the JAAF 4th Air Army, showing many of the bomber, reconnaissance and transport units featured in this volume.

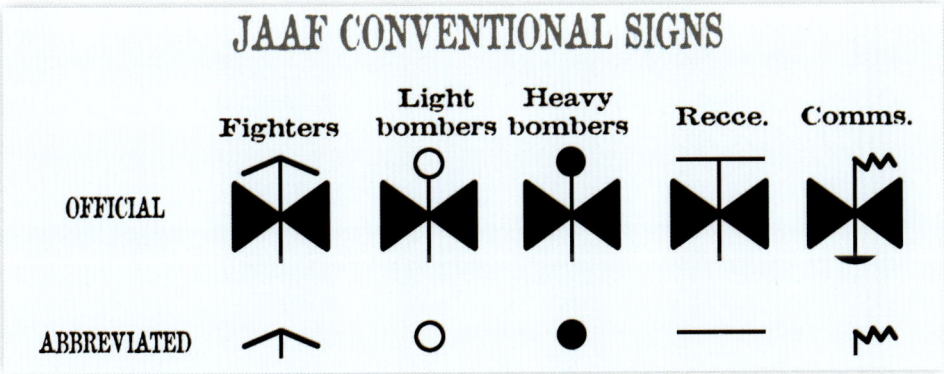

JAAF symbols and abbreviations used to describe particular types of air unit.

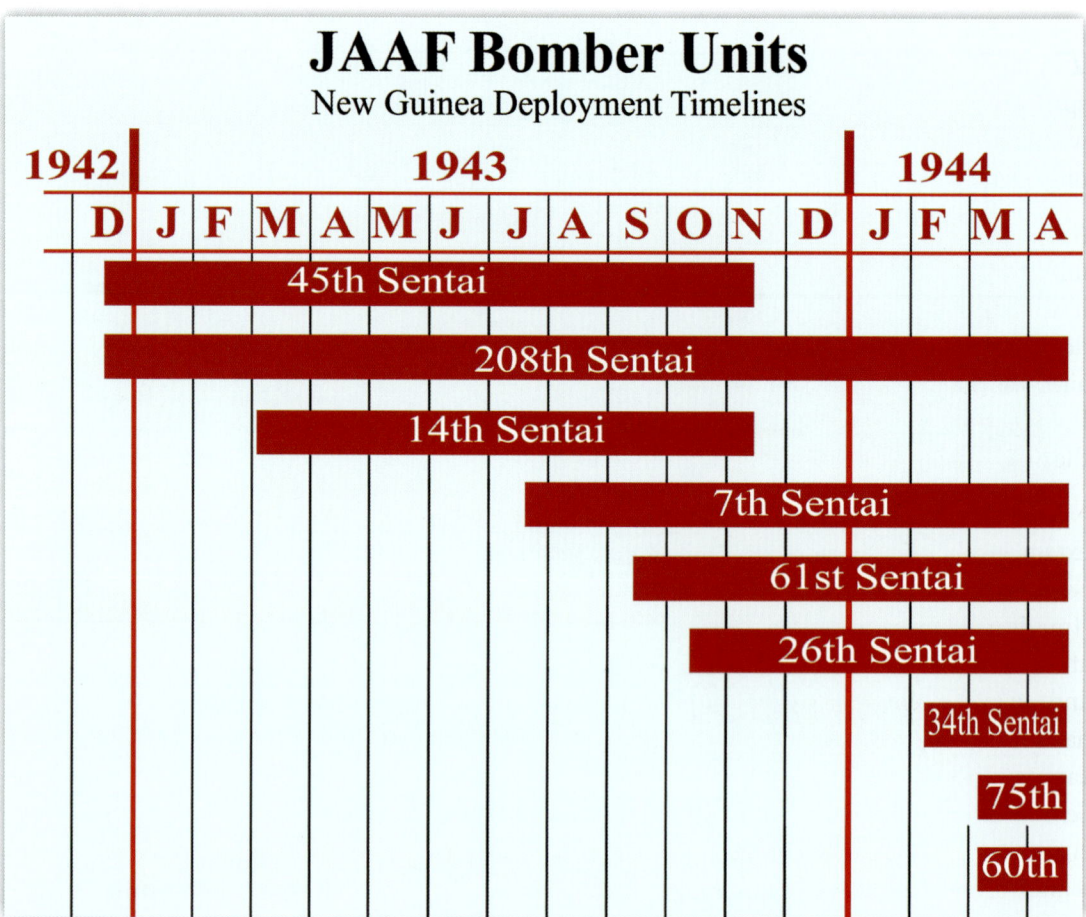

A diagram showing the timeframe of New Guinea deployments for the nine JAAF bomber units featured in this volume.

CHAPTER 1
JAAF Bombers and Support Types in the South Pacific

As outlined in *Pacific Profiles Volume One*, in late 1942 the Southeast Area was remote from the occupied minds of JAAF command. JAAF reluctance to commit its increasingly thinly spread resources stemmed from the consideration that neither its training, equipment nor doctrine was suited to such a vast tropical theatre. Already engaged in a protracted war in Asia, its robust opposition to deployment to the remote South Pacific theatre was both sensible and justified.

It is understandable then that the first JAAF air unit to arrive at Rabaul was a reconnaissance unit, the 76th Independent Reconnaissance *Chutai*, transferred from the Philippines. When it arrived on 12 October 1942, at this early stage a cautious JAAF still had time to make sea deliveries. However later on due to combat pressures this amenity was removed, costing many airframes and lives during long delivery flights. In late 1943 after much mulling and debate, an IJN-IJA inaugural agreement was ratified on air operations in New Guinea, New Britain and the Solomons, committing the 6th *Hikoshidan* (Air Division) to the Southeast theatre.

Neither is it surprising that the first two JAAF bomber units to be sent to the theatre had been extensively trained in remote-area navigation. Both the 45th *Sentai* and its sister unit the 208th *Sentai* fell under the command of the Hakujoshi Operational Training *Hikodan*. However, the "training" designation is deceptive as both *sentai* were combat units, whose aircrew were adept at navigation over featureless desert. Hakujoshi was located on the central Manchuria plain, and was thus central to extensive and featureless geography. In December 1942 the 45th *Sentai* had twenty Ki-48 *Sokei* light bombers delivered as deck cargo directly to Rabaul (onboard the carrier *Zuikaku*) and it became the first JAAF bomber unit to operate in the theatre. The 208th *Sentai* soon followed, attempting the final Truk to Rabaul sector by air. On 3 May 1943 the entire regiment of 45 Lily bombers, escorted by about a dozen new Navy Zeros, attempted the flight but were forced to return because of a weather front. The regiment sat out nearly a week at Truk anticipating the weather to clear, and made a second delivery attempt on 9 May 1943, safely arriving at Rabaul (Vunakanau) that afternoon. Two days later they flew the last leg to their new home of Dagua near Wewak. Both units served under the umbrella of the Hakujoshi "training" *Hikodan* throughout their New Guinea deployments.

The 4th Air Army in New Guinea had yet to be formed when these initial JAAF bomber units assigned to the 6th *Hikoshidan* commanded by Lieutenant-General Itahana Gi'ichi arrived at Rabaul from Manchuria. Due to the massive increase in Allied air opposition a new air army – the 4th Air Army - was created in August 1943 led by Lieutenant-General Teramoto Kumaichi. This new army was created by redeploying 7th *Hikoshidan* units from Java and the Netherlands East Indies (led by Lieutenant-General Sudo Einosuke) and joining them with Itahana's 6th *Hikoshidan*. On 25 March 43, a final IJN-JAAF agreement was finally reached which assigned primary responsibilities within the theatre; the JAAF would cover New Guinea, and the IJN the Solomons. However, once again combat demands saw both services represented in both areas.

On 4 July 1943 sixteen 14th *Sentai* Ki-21 bombers bombed US forces invading New Georgia, escorted by seventeen 1st *Sentai Hayabusa* and 49 Zeros from Buin. Six Ki-21s were shot down, and two more forced landed at Ballale. A rare burst of inter-service cooperation saw JAAF fighters share the responsibility of escort with their IJN counterparts, but the bomber losses were such the JAAF refused to return to the Solomons. These were the last major operations by the JAAF in the Solomons, and thereafter the two services adhered, more or less, to the agreement. Shortly after becoming established on mainland New Guinea low-level strafing attacks wiped out the major cadre of JAAF units, especially the bombers which were hard to hide and which offered themselves as lucrative targets.

On 26 December 1943 JAAF bombers were once again drawn into major conflict alongside their IJN counterparts, this time with Ki-49 *Donryu* heavy bombers from the 7th and 61st *Sentai*. Again another disastrous loss of six *Donryu* near Cape Gloucester resulted in a change to operational policy. *Donryu* would no longer fly daytime missions in New Guinea. Instead, the type would be confined to night-time supply drops and bombing raids, neither of which would arrest the declining fortunes of the despairing IJA in New Guinea. Instead, five 7th *Sentai* bombers were put into service as mail couriers running frequent runs between Ambon, Manila, Wakde, But, Alexishafen, Wewak and Rabaul, while the handful of other surviving *Donryu* was ordered back to Japan on 17 January 1944. All surplus aircrew were transferred to the 61st *Sentai* so it could maintain operational strength. By the time the *sentai* returned to Hamamatsu, Japan, in February 1944, the 7th *Sentai* had lost 87 aircrew to New Guinea operations, at a cost of incurring negligible damage to the enemy. It is telling that the premier JAAF heavy bomber unit, which had arrived in New Guinea with the promise of taking the offensive, wound up conducting mail delivery instead.

A vast array of dedicated transport units operated throughout mainland New Guinea conducting logistics, communications and liaison flights throughout the theatre. This included former heavy bombers as outlined above and included host of small independent transport flights directly commanded by 4th Air Army Headquarters. Also in the mix were the civilian companies Japan Aviation and Southern Air Corporation. The Tachikawa Air Transport Department and the Army Air Evaluation Section also visited infrequently, while the 8th Army Headquarters operated its own detachment of two Ki-57s. Other miscellaneous units which operated throughout the theatre included communications units and the 1st Air Route detachment. Thus, an eclectic mix of Ki-21s, Ki-49s, Ki-57s, LC-20s and Ki-56s (a licence-built Lockheed Model 14 Super Electra) all saw service in this busy theatre.

From its formation until its collapse at Wewak in 1944, the 4th Air Army lost 710 aircraft, of which only 225 of which were lost to air combat. The majority of 373 were destroyed on the ground by Allied attacks while 112 were lost to other causes, primarily accidents due to poor airfield conditions. Airfields were repaired after air raid damage, in most cases simply to ensure self-survival, let alone to continue operations. Towards the end defensive units were given priority for scarce fuel supplies. All JAAF commanders were continually berated by their Tokyo seniors for losses to Allied bombings. In the end, JAAF command kept throwing replacement aircraft at a campaign they could not win.

Yet, the final chapter for JAAF bomber operations is both curious and peculiar. On their way to invading Hollandia in April 1944, the Allies deliberately by-passed Wewak and its satellite airfields, not captured until May 1945 by Australian troops. This meant large sections of General Adachi Hatazo's 18th Army were left to fend for themselves. On an unknown date in January 1945, a Ki-21 transport bomber flew in from Java a planeload of supplies for the 115th Infantry Brigade around Wewak. It used a makeshift field prepared on Cape Wom which had escaped the attention of Allied intelligence. It landed late in the afternoon from which an army officer with rank of Captain was driven straight to 25th Army Battalion headquarters to deliver critical medical supplies. It departed early the next morning. This was the last JAAF aerial operation conducted on mainland New Guinea.

CHAPTER 2
Technical Notes

Many types and different models of bombers, transports, reconnaissance aircraft, attack aircraft and their variants served with the JAAF in New Guinea. The main types being the Ki-49-I and II *Donryu* heavy bomber, Ki-21-I and II heavy bomber and derivative MC-21 transport, Ki-51 attack and reconnaissance aircraft, Ki-48-I and II *Sokei* light bomber, Ki-46-II reconnaissance aircraft, and Ki-57 & Ki-56 transports. Some types such as the Tachikawa Ki-55 trainer and Mansyu Ki-79 trainer made cameo appearances but are not discussed further in this chapter due to their rarity. The technical summaries below focus where possible on the operational eccentricities of each type in respect to New Guinea operations. Note that none of the "heavy" bombers would have earned that classification under any Allied guidelines.

Note that the *ko* 甲, *otsu* 乙, and *hei* 丙 suffixes as applied by JAAF Headquarters to *Kitai* numbers (abbreviated as *Ki*) usually designate armament modifications. These suffixes have been almost universally rendered in English publications as "a", "b" and "c" variants. However, these designations are a retrospective convenience, invented from the ordinal *kanji*, used only in English literature and never by the manufacturers themselves. Note also that the Japanese Army designated any automatic weapon with a calibre above 11 mm as a "machine cannon". Ammunition used in theatre for 7.7mm weapons was a mixture of standard ball and tracer, with Armour-Piercing (AP), High Explosive (HE), and HE tracer used by 12.7 mm "machine cannon".

Sally - Mitsubishi Ki-21-I and II Heavy Bomber

Classified as a heavy bomber, the first models from the Ki-21-I through to the Ki-21-II-*ko* were discernible by an elongated dorsal "glasshouse". Whilst many of these glasshouse variants served in theatre as transports, the vast majority deployed on combat operations in New Guinea were Ki-21-II-*otsu* which also served in the transport role, usually with a crew of five. The type, code-named Sally, was liked by its aircrews for its ease of maintenance and good handling, often being preferred to its replacement, the Ki-49 *Donryu*.

Dinah - Ki-46-II Reconnaissance Aircraft

Such was its prowess that Mitsubishi's Ki-46, code-named Dinah, became the only type to eventually serve with both the IJN and JAAF. With a tandem crew separated by a fuel tank, its weakest point was its undercarriage strength, and collapses persisted throughout its service life. The observer's seat was on a lengthy sliding rail, with the camera located in front of the observer. Although there was provision for the observer to mount a defensive 7.7mm machine gun, this was commonly omitted in New Guinea along with the ring mount. Only the Ki-46-II was operated in New Guinea, although later in the war Hollandia was visited by the occasional Ki-46-III on liaison duties.

The type was used almost exclusively for long-range reconnaissance, including surveillance and photography where it cruised comfortably at higher altitudes at 215 knots. As the war wore on, it was increasingly used for liaison purposes including the delivery of dispatches between Hollandia, Rabaul and Wewak, and transport of some essential supplies. Patrols of up to five hours duration and up to 30,000 feet enabled pilots to take advantage of tailwinds to make distance. There are many times where Allied fighters tried unsuccessfully to reach Ki-46s, and anti-aircraft guns rarely brought one down unless it strayed into lower altitudes. Instead, most losses were weather-related or operational.

Unit ground staff loaded and serviced reconnaissance cameras, with supporting Airfield Battalion units processing undeveloped film. Interpretation of photography was made in the first instance by unit headquarters' detachments, before forwarding to higher authority. Ground crew would normally warm up Ki-46 engines before missions. It only took approximately ten minutes to refuel a Ki-46 from a tanker truck. Engines were rarely replaced in the field as they were not put under stress.

Lily - Kawasaki Ki-48-II *ko*, *otsu* and *hei Sokei* Light Bomber

Although a handful of Ki-48-Is served in New Guinea the vast majority were Ki-48-II *ko* and *otsu* models. This later model was almost identical to its predecessor but had upgraded engines and aircrew armour plating. The *otsu* was built as a dive-bomber with retractable dive brakes. However, these were never used operationally in the theatre and were usually removed altogether to save weight. The Ki-48-II *hei* later also served in the theatre, incorporating armament improvements.

Units operating the *Sokei*, code-named Lily, in New Guinea nicknamed it *satsujinki* (suicide plane). Its shortfalls included ineffective bomb load, poor manoeuvrability, slow speed and a slow rate of climb. The magnetos regularly faltered or failed, and the machine guns had limited azimuth of fire, making it vulnerable to fighters. In New Guinea the effect of the Ki-48 against Allied ground targets proved almost negligible.

Helen - Nakajima Ki-49-I and II Heavy Bomber/ Transport

The first army bomber fitted with a tail turret, the Ki-49 Type 100 heavy bomber was officially named *Donryu* in honour of the Shinto shrine in Ota prefecture near the factory where it was built. Code-named Helen, it was nicknamed "dragon eater", in a smug and officially encouraged reference to the obsolescent USAAF B-23 Dragon bomber, which the Japanese viewed as inferior. Although the Ki-49 was the JAAF's biggest bomber, it would not have qualified as a heavy bomber under any Allied classification.

To improve take-off performance the bomber was equipped with fowler flaps, inspired by the Lockheed airliners for which the Japanese had a license to build. The Ki-49 also had a unique extra-wide inner wing chord to hold fuel tanks. The *Donryu* was revealed to the Japanese media during an inaugural flight over Tokyo in January 1943, however the acquisition soon proved disappointing; its speed proved little better than the Ki-21 Sally bomber which it replaced, and it toted a lesser payload. On New Guinea airfields its crew members often positioned themselves forward for take-offs in order to move the centre of gravity forward. This could be critical during take-offs on damaged airfields of limited length. Furthermore, the Ki-49's role in the theatre was curtailed by poor serviceability and lack of spares.

The IJA sent *Donryu* to New Guinea to provide an offensive capability in the theatre, part of which were plans to attack Port Moresby as a priority target. However, Ki-49s only got there once – on 20 September 1943 – when four launched from Dagua in evening heavy rain. Stormy conditions forced two to turn back, one of which ditched offshore drowning the five crew. Only two Ki-49s got through, rendering but slight damage to the target. The lackluster mission marked the final Japanese air-raid against the town for the entire war, and the final offensive *Donryu* mission in New Guinea. Despite the paltry results, Tokyo radio described the alleged successful mission of two bombers as a "mass formation".

While the Ki-49-II-*otsu* was the most common type to serve in theatre, a handful of Ki-49-Is remained in service with the 61st *Sentai* throughout. In the end, Allied bombing and strafing raids destroyed more *Donryu* than aerial encounters, and towards the end of its New Guinea service it was performing exclusively in the transport role.

Sonia- Mitsubishi Ki-51 Reconnaissance and Attack Aircraft

The Ki-51 codenamed Sonia was designed as a ground attack aircraft with emphasis placed on manoeuvrability and ability to operate from crude airfields close to the front line. A small bombload of 200 kilograms was carried via a fuselage-mounted shackle. One 7.7mm machine gun was installed in the observer's position for aircraft protection, with a 7.7mm machine gun installed in each wing. Leading edge slats improved performance and handling at low speed, and later models had armour plating around the cockpit area and engine bay.

The type was easily converted in the field to alternate between attack or reconnaissance roles, including installation of a camera on the top surface of the starboard wing. As the war progressed in New Guinea it was also much used in a liaison capacity, which included the carriage of VIPs. Its most critical passenger was the commander of the 18th Army, General Adachi Hatazo, who was flown from Madang to Salamaua on 2 and 3 August 1943, as outlined in the unit history of the 83rd Independent *Chutai*.

The Ki-51 was liked by its crews as it was easy to fly and maintain. In New Guinea it often operated alone and rarely attracted attention from Allied fighters. On the rare occasions when it did, it was usually erroneously identified as either a Zeke, Oscar or even a Val.

Thalia - Kawasaki Ki-56 Transport

After receiving a license to build the Lockheed 14 civilian airliner, Kawasaki was tasked to improve the type into a troop transport by increasing cabin space and boosting take-off performance. The fuselage was increased by about one and a half metres, the wings were lightened in structure, lighter engines were fitted, and a larger cargo door was installed. The type, codenamed Thalia, was eventually used in every theatre of Japanese operations, and in New Guinea was seen at Wewak, Rabaul and Hollandia.

Sally - Mitsubishi Ki-57 / MC-20 and MC-21 Transport

The Mitsubishi MC-21 was a transport aircraft converted from obsolete Ki-21-I inventory withdrawn from combat. They were operated by a crew of four and carried a normal passenger load of nine. It was an interim design pending the arrival of the Ki-57 / MC-20, the purpose-built transport based on the Ki-21. The MC-21 airframe had all military equipment and armament removed with the dorsal greenhouse faired over, whereas the Ki-57 has a purpose-built civilian airframe with passenger windows. All variants operated in the New Guinea theatre.

A 7th Sentai early model Ki-49-II taxies at Dagua after landing with Fowler flaps deployed.

A good example of overall green as applied to several early batches at Ki-49-II at Hamamatsu. (courtesy Darryl Ford)

CHAPTER 3
The 7th *Hiko Sentai*

The 7th *Sentai* was was the Imperial Army's oldest heavy bomber unit. It was stationed in Manchuria at the outbreak of the Pacific War operating Ki-21s and became the second unit to covert to the Nakajima Ki-49-I *Donryu* heavy bomber after the 61st *Sentai*. Both units were assigned to the 9th *Hikodan* (Flying Brigade).

In early 1942 the 7th *Sentai* moved to Java then Surabaya before returning to Japan where it converted to the upgraded model Ki-49-II at Hamamatsu training base. While undertaking conversion training there, on 19 June 1943 the unit was unexpectedly ordered to Wewak in order to support the 18th Army under Lieutenant-General Adachi Hatazo. The commander of the 7th *Sentai* originally resisted the deployment due to the poor condition of New Guinea airfields, arguing they were unsuitable for the heavy bombers. Nonetheless the move proceeded with a total of 35 bombers moving to the new theare. The bombers were first shipped to Truk, reassembled, and then guided by an IJN G4M1 bomber to Rabaul. The unit was taken to New Guinea by their new commander, Major Toyokichi Ohnishi, the first bombers arriving at Dagua on 24 July 1943. The type was first noted in New Guinea by Allied intelligence when fourteen were photographed at Dagua the week later, with about half left behind at Rapopo airfield near Rabaul. By end of August 1943 most *Donryu* had made their way to But and Dagua airfields.

The 7th *Sentai*'s first target was Mount Hagen in the New Guinea highlands where the Japanese suspected that the Allies were developing a major airbase. This occurred on 12 August 1943 when twenty 7th *Sentai Donryu*, escorted by 59th *Sentai* Ki-43-II *Hayabusa*, bombed the area. Two days later seven *Donryu* bombed Wau, and on 15 August the first *Donryu* was lost on operations during a night attack against the new USAAF airbase at Marilinan in a mountainous valley behind Lae. In September 1943, the No. 1 *Chutai* led by Captain Suzuki Masanori successfully bombed US forces at Sattleberg.

No Japanese, let alone any member of the 7th *Sentai*, foresaw the disaster which arrived on their doorstep on 17 August 1943 in the form of low-level Mitchell attackers. These field-modified strafers removed fourteen heavy bombers from the unit's inventory of twenty serviceable *Donryu* at Wewak. By the end of September, the 7th *Sentai* had been reduced to only three serviceable *Donryu*. Although piecemeal replacements kept arriving, for offensive missions it henceforth combined forces with the 61st *Sentai* to make up numbers.

Due to ongoing Allied air raids, the situation at But and Wewak airfields deteriorated further with limited aircraft spares brought in by Daihatsu barges or submarines at night. Malaria and dengue fever also took toll on many JAAF units, including the 7th *Sentai*, and lack of clean drinking water gave widespread diarrhoea. In November 1943 *chutaicho* Lieutenant Endo Tsutomo died of malaria, an ailment which had also claimed the life of unit commander, Major Toyokichi Ohnishi, who had brought the unit to New Guinea. With only a handful of bombers

This Donryu showcases the "snake weave" pattern common in 7th Sentai ranks at Dagua.

left, operations were now confined to night operations, with the limited number of bombers deployed to drop supplies to isolated detachments of IJA soldiers. Two 7th *Sentai Donryu* flew the last raid against Port Moresby on evening of 20 September 1943. By October 1943 its inventory listed nine bombers, with an average of four to five airworthy on most days. On 12 December 1943 three 7th *Sentai Donryu* were lost during an attack against Nadzab, and another five were lost three days later when attacking Arawe. On 26 December the disastrous loss of six 9th *Hikodan Donryu* shook both *sentai* commanders and resulted in a landmark change to operational policy. *Donryu* would no longer fly daytime missions in New Guinea. Instead, the type would be confined to night-time supply drops and bombing raids, neither of which would arrest the declining fortunes of the despairing Japanese Army in New Guinea.

The unit's last supply mission in New Guinea was flown on 8 January 1944 by a pair of *Donryu* against Finschhafen. This was led by Lieutenant Ugakami who failed to return in poor weather. Meanwhile five serviceable 7th *Sentai* bombers were put into service as army mail couriers running frequent flights between Ambon, Manila, Wakde, But, Alexishafen, Wewak and Rabaul. The handful of remaining *Donryu* was ordered back to Japan on 17 January 1944.

After departure of all the unit's *Donryu* from New Guinea, all surplus aircrew were transferred to the 61st *Sentai* so this unit could maintain operational strength. By the time the *sentai* returned to Hamamatsu, Japan, in February 1944, it had lost 87 aircrew while undertaking New Guinea operations. Back home, the unit was re-equipped with the modern Ki-67 *Hiryu* bomber. Whilst the New Guinea deployment at first held high hope that the type would contribute a sorely lacking aerial offensive capability in the theatre, in the end after many losses the *Donryu* barely contributed to Japanese objectives.

The striking unit motif for the 7th Sentai is displayed on two late model Donryu tails at Hollandia just before capture.

Photographed at Dagua on 22 October 1943, the yellow trim tab indicates a No. 3 Chutai bomber.

Markings

Most of the original batch of early model Ki-49-IIs flown to Rabaul were painted at Hamamatsu in a variety of schemes, including overall green, a two-tone camouflage or a variety of wave patterns. The two-tone scheme emulated the *kumogata* scheme (cloud-style), previously used extensively over China.

During the initial deployment no unit insignia was applied but some pilots named their aircraft after different bird species; two confirmed examples are hawk (鷹) as in Profile 5 and eagle (鷲), usually hand-painted on the upper fin in *kanji*. Rudder trim tabs were also painted in *chutai* colours of white, red and yellow to differentiate between the Nos. 1, 2 and 3 *chutai* respectively. Later during the campaign names of cities and mountains were also used, two examples being Ito (伊東) and Muramatsu (村松).

Combat experience earned in the Southeast area led to the final production model Ki-49-II-*otsu* which included heavier defensive machine guns and two extra windows installed to the waist defensive gun position. These bombers were all painted in different types of camouflage weave including snake-weave patterns applied at Hamamatsu training base before leaving for New Guinea. These later models also adopted the highly visible unit tail motif based on the English numeral seven. This markings system was introduced around late 1943 and *chutai* colours were changed to blue, red or yellow to represent the Nos. 1, 2 or 3 *Chutai* respectively.

Abandoned bomb stocks used by Donryu captured at Hollandia.

Three-Way Profile

This unusual mottled camouflage scheme was seen on a No. 3 Chutai Ki-49 at Hollandia. Note that the white combat fuselage band has red piping.

PACIFIC PROFILES

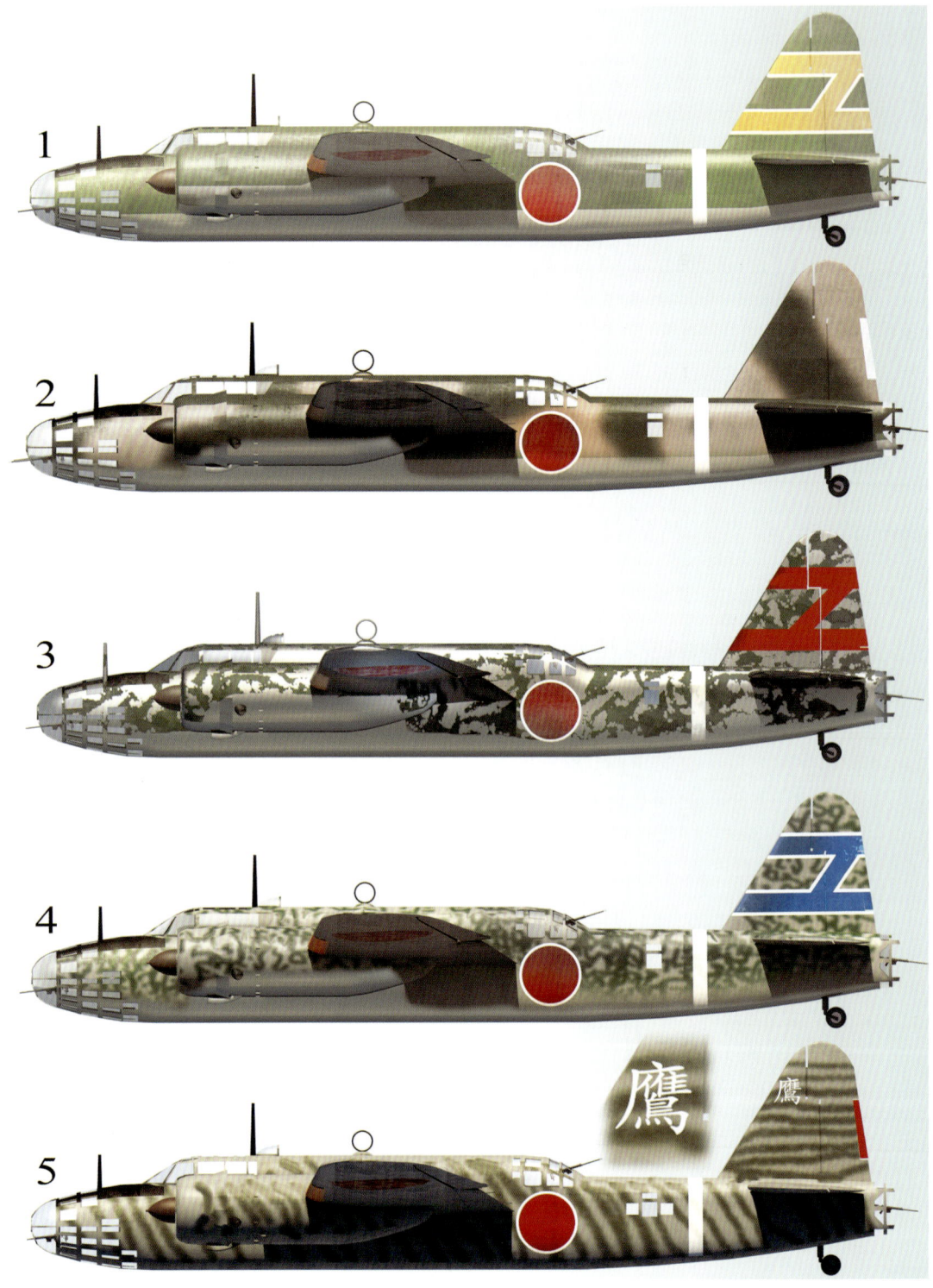

Profiles 1–5 (Ki-49 *Donryu* / Helen)

1. This No. 3 *Chutai* overall green camouflage early model Ki-49-II (single waist gun port) was captured at Hollandia in April 1944.

2. A photo of an early model Ki-49-II (single waist gun port) departing Japan for New Guinea showcases a two-tone *kumogata* scheme previously used extensively over China. Although an early *Donryu* scheme, several examples of this scheme were also found on wrecked *Donryu* at Hollandia (Sentani) when captured by the Allies in April 1944. The colours are referenced from the colour photo of a Ki-49 wreck in the Philippines with the same scheme (see the photo at the bottom of this page).

3. This No. 2 *Chutai* green-sprayed weave camouflage late model Ki-49-II was captured at Hollandia in April 1944. Such camouflage schemes were applied at Hamamatsu training base with a spray gun set at medium pressure, prior to departure for New Guinea. Note the unit insignia lacks white piping.

4. This No. 1 *Chutai* green-sprayed squiggly camouflage early model Ki-49-II was captured at Hollandia in April 1944.

5. The "zebra" camouflage scheme was applied at Hamamatsu to a batch of late model Ki-49-II just prior to departure for New Guinea via Tainan and the Philippines, the later preferred delivery route. This photo is referenced from an air-to-air photo of the same. This bomber has a red No. 2 *Chutai* trim tab and the *kanji* character "hawk" (鷹) painted on the fin as seen at Hollandia in March 1944.

This two-tone kumogata early scheme used originally over China was seen on several Ki-49-II at Hollandia. This Donryu wreck in the Philippines has the same scheme, the colours of which are used as a reference for Profile 2. (courtesy Darryl Ford)

The subject of Profile 11 as captured at Lae in September 1943. The dark band forward of the hinomaru is not a painted marking but is instead separate panelling.

CHAPTER 4
The 14th *Hiko Sentai*

The 14th *Sentai* was equipped with Ki-21 bombers when it left Malang, Java, on 24 February 1943 to fly all the way to Rapopo near Rabaul. The six-day delivery flight proceeded via Kendari, Babo and Wewak and saw the bombers arrive at Rapopo on 2 March 1943. Although a bomber unit, between combat missions the 14th *Sentai* was constantly involved in transport, liaison and supply duties, and would continue to do so throughout its New Guinea deployment. Its first mission was on 9 March when 26 Ki-21s bombed the mountain valley town of Wau. In a rare show of IJN / JAAF cooperation, they were escorted by eighteen No. 253 *Kokutai* Zeros. On 24 March the unit conducted its first major transport mission, repatriating about thirty 18th Army staff officers from Lae back to Rabaul whose vessels had been sunk during the Battle of the Bismarck Sea earlier that month.

The unit's bombers flew three night bombing missions against Oro bay in late March, however the unit had started facing another adversary. Only a month after having arrived in theatre many aircrew succumbed to malaria and dengue fever. This debilitated the unit's effectiveness throughout the New Guinea campaign, as indeed were all other 4th Air Army units similarly afflicted. In April commanding officer Lieutenant Colonel Itoda (first name unknown) was transferred to another theatre in a staff role and replaced by Major Endo Misao. In June the unit bombed the New Guinea highlands at Bena Bena, however misfortune was about to materialise when it was instructed to become involved in the Rendova campaign in the Solomon Islands.

The first Rendova mission was led by Endo on 2 July with eighteen Ki-21s. Two days later Endo returned with sixteen Ki-21s, escorted by seventeen 1st *Sentai* Ki-43-I *Hayabusa* and a fighter force of 49 Zeros based at Buin. The Zeros reached Rendova first feinting an approach to the south where they became entangled in a major battle with Allied fighters. Meanwhile Endo's bombers, flying at 13,000 feet, approached the island from the southeast, turned right and conducted a northeast bombing run. The bombs hit many ships but 90mm heavy flak and enemy fighters cost six Ki-21s shot down. The escorting *Hayabusa* lost three, with two pilots rescued. Due to such heavy losses the JAAF decided the unit would fly no more missions in the Solomons.

On 12 August 22 Ki-21-IIs bombed Mount Hagen, and two days later returned to Wau this time with seven bombers. The devastating low-level Mitchell strafing raid of 17 August against Wewak's airfields destroyed three 14th *Sentai* bombers on the ground. Two consecutive raids were made against Nadzab on afternoon of 20 September, each with nine Ki-21-IIs. For the rest of the month the unit's bombers attacked Finschhafen with limited success. Meanwhile the 14th *Sentai* had still maintained a presence at Rapopo, and during the 12 October 1943 low-level attack against the base, *chutaicho* Lieutenant Yusada Norito and crew were killed when their Ki-21-II was shot down by a strafing 345th BG Mitchell.

In between combat missions the unit's bombers continued to ferry supplies and men. On 25 October 1943 a trio of bombers was lost in bad weather while returning to Rabaul from Manila in the Philippines, including the unit's executive officer Major Ishikawa Masayasu. On 6 November the Wewak contingent advanced to Madang from where they planned a series of attacks against Nadzab. On 7 November a squadron of Warhawks fell into the bomber formation as it approached Nadzab. Two Ki-21-IIs were shot down, piloted by Lieutenants Tarasawa Toshio and Fukuda Shigeo. Lieutenant Kawakita Shozo ditched his badly shot-up bomber off the northern New Guinea coast, with the loss of two crew.

Subsequent to this mission JAAF command considered that the 14th *Sentai* no longer had sufficient strength to maintain an offensive role. Accordingly, they were ordered westwards to Namlea 'drome in West New Guinea. From here for the next two months they patrolled the Banda Strait.

Markings

All Mitsubishi Ki-21 bombers left the factory painted in an overall light grey. Camouflage was later applied in the field and varied from overall shades of green to varieties of weave and splotch patterns, unique to each aircraft. The unit insignia derives from an artistic interpretation of the English numbers 1 and 4. Each bomber received an individual aircraft number, usually painted on the lower portion of the rudder. These appear to have been assigned on a consecutive basis, as each aircraft was received by the unit. The 14th *Sentai* used the colours white, red and yellow for the Nos. 1, 2 and 3 *Chutai* respectively. It is possible that blue was applied to the headquarters detachment, however no evidence for this has surfaced. Some tail motifs applied thin white piping to accentuate the insignia from the camouflage.

Evidenced by the remnants of a white insignia on the fin, here are the remains of a No. 1 Chutai Ki-21-II at Hollandia, one of the few colour photos of the type in New Guinea. (courtesy Darryl Ford)

THE 14TH HIKO SENTAI

The tail of Ki-21-II #45 which was left intact when the Japanese abandoned the Madang / Alexishafen airfields. The wooden component at the bottom of the rudder is a control lock, and camouflage netting covers the tailplane.

This angle from a low-level strike photo shows clearly the combination of field camouflage and tail insignia which denoted most of the unit's bombers. Two "parafrag" bombs are visible, which were liberally dispersed during the low-level Fifth Air Force raids.

The tail of a wrecked No. 3 Chutai bomber at Hollandia. In the background are A-20Gs assigned to the 312th BG.

PACIFIC PROFILES

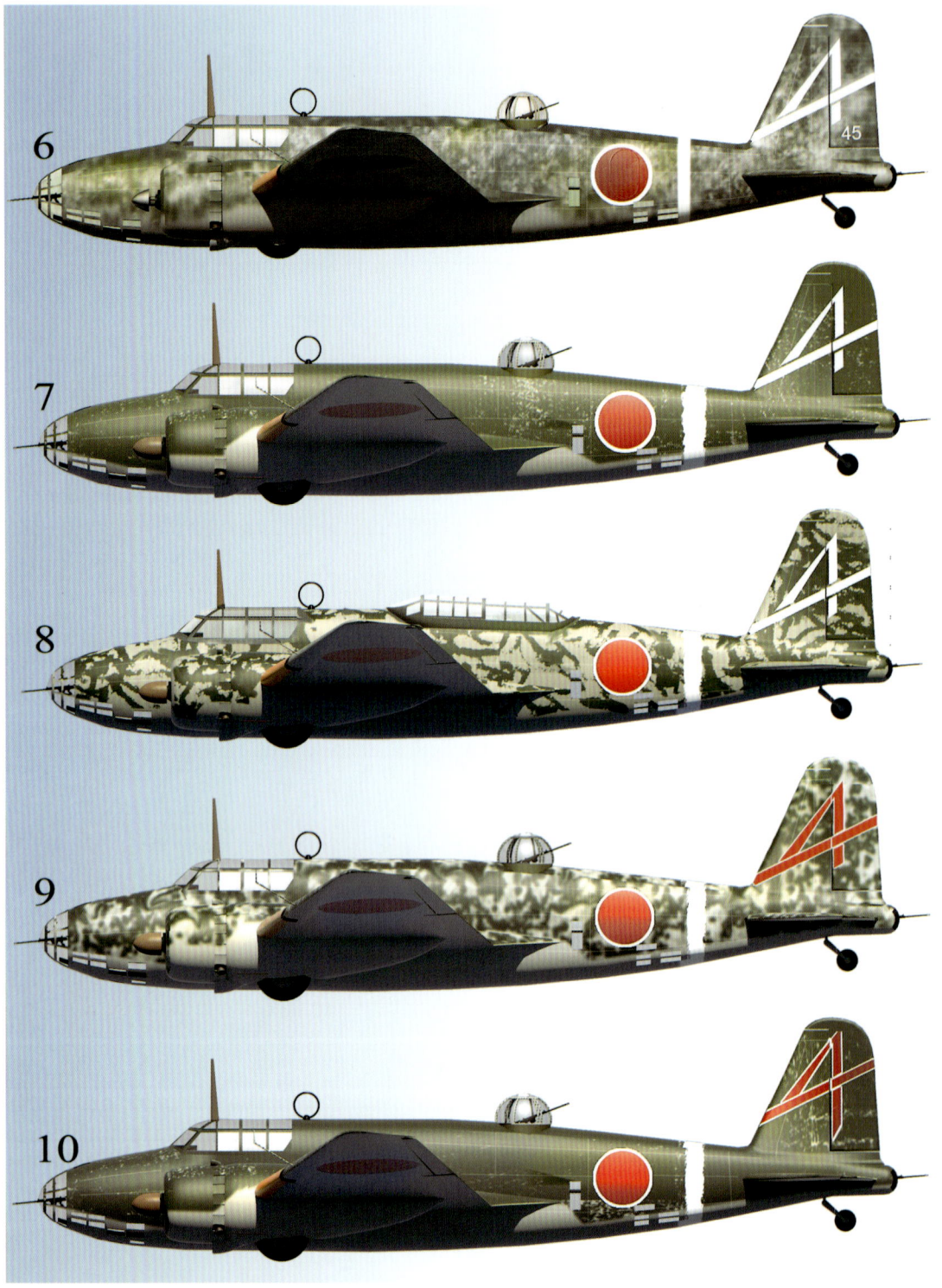

Profiles 6-10 (Ki-21 Sally)

6. Ki-21-II # 45 assigned to the No. 1 *Chutai*, was captured completely intact in the Madang / Alexishafen area in April 1944. The aircraft number 45 suggests that at least 45 Ki-21s served with the 14th *Sentai* up until the time it left New Guinea.

7. Ki-21-II MN 4335, No. 1 *Chutai*. This bomber was one of sixteen Ki-21s which departed Rapopo near Rabaul to bomb the American beachhead at Munda on 4 July 1943, escorted by 1st *Sentai Hayabusa* and IJN Zeros. Over the target they were met with anti-aircraft fire and intercepted by Allied fighters. This bomber was hit in both engines and forced-landed back at Ballale where it was abandoned. Another Ki-21 from the No. 2 *Chutai* also forced-landed at Ballale flown by Lieutenant Takayama (first name unrecorded).

8. Ki-21-I, No. 1 *Chutai*. This early model Ki-21 with the dorsal "bird-cage" was photographed at Lakunai in late 1943. The 14th *Sentai* used these early model bombers for transport purposes.

9. Ki-21-II, No. 2 *Chutai*. Also a participant on the same 4 July 1943 raid as described in Profile 7, this bomber later ditched off a small island to the northwest of Munda. An AA burst over the target badly wounded the pilot Corporal Kanamori (first name unrecorded) in the stomach who slumped over the controls. Engineer Sergeant Nakaide (first name unrecorded) tried to extinguish a fire which had started in the fuselage. With the port engine blown off, aircraft commander Lieutenant Nakayama (first name unrecorded) took over the controls and ditched the bomber on the way back to Rabaul.

Shortly after the crew made it to the shore the bomber exploded. Although successfully taken to dry land, the badly wounded pilot Kanamori shortly thereafter took his own life with a pistol. Japanese soldiers from an observation outpost radioed the crew's location to Rabaul. A few days later they were collected by the destroyer *Harukaze*, then transferred to the cruiser *Chokai* which returned them to Rabaul on 8 July 1943.

10. Ki-21-II MN 6382, No. 2 *Chutai*. This bomber was one of the survivors of a costly mission on 7 November 1943 when nine Ki-21s escorted by the 13th and 248th *Sentai* bombed Nadzab from around 20,000 feet. Four bombers were shot down by Allied fighters and five made forced landings at Alexishafen. Two days later Allied strafers claimed five bombers destroyed when they attacked the field.

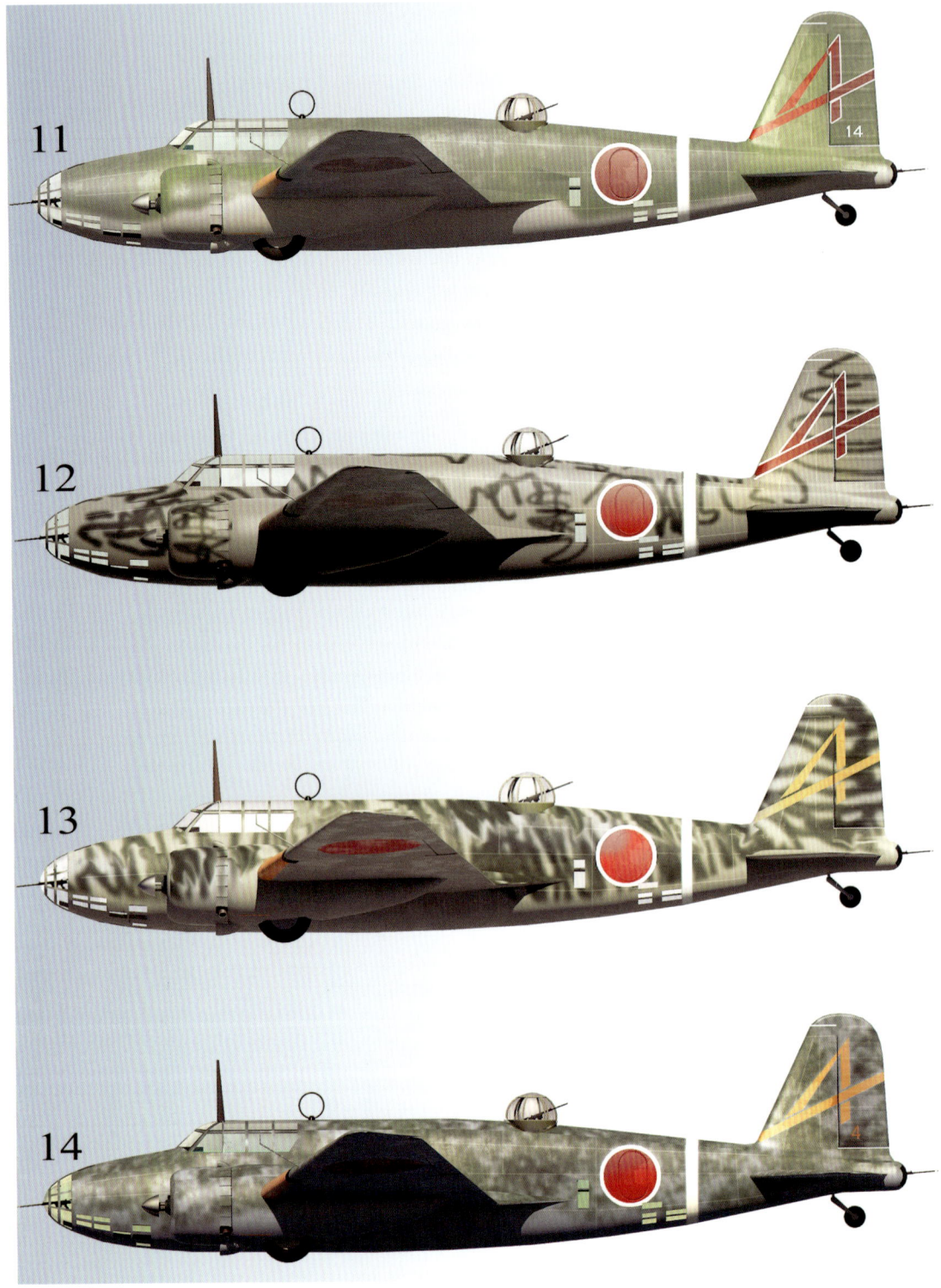

Profiles 11-14 (Ki-21 Sally)

11. Ki-21-II MN 4318 #14 was assigned to the No. 2 *Chutai* and was captured at Lae in September 1943. Piping is only evident on the rudder portion of the motif, suggesting this was a replacement part.

12. Ki-21-II assigned to the No. 2 *Chutai* that was captured at Hollandia in April 1944.

13. Ki-21-II assigned to the No. 3 *Chutai* that served at Rapopo, Rabaul, in October 1943.

14. Ki-21-II MN 6323 #4 assigned to the No. 3 *Chutai*. It was shot down near Nadzab on 7 November 1943, while flown by Lieutenant Tarasawa Toshio. The Allied field report on this wreck notes that the undercoat paint was a light blue. This reflects an early camouflage scheme used in the China theatre.

The subject of Profile 12 as wrecked and captured at Hollandia in April 1944.

The subject of the Three-Way Profile as abandoned on But 'drome's coastline in airworthy condition.

CHAPTER 5
The 26th *Hiko Sentai*

Classified as a light bomber / attack unit, the 26th *Sentai* only operated Ki-51s in the New Guinea theatre, despite some accounts stating they also operated *Hayabusa* there. Both the No. 2 and 3 *Chutai* were deployed from Clark Field, Luzon, to But airfield on 23 October 1943 under the command of the No. 3 *chutaicho* Captain Takano Kunihiko. These two *chutai* were equipped with the Mitsubishi Ki-51 and their assigned tasks focused on mounting ground attack missions and reconnaissance patrols, mainly in support of the 18th Army.

On 9 November a detachment of five of the No. 3 *Chutai*'s later-model Ki-51s moved to Alexishafen. These airframes had additional armour-plating, additional fuel tanks and hard-points to carry up to 200 kilograms of bombs under the wings. A few days after the Alexishafen detachment arrived, it was ordered to Cape Gloucester (Japanese name Tuluvu), from where it conducted alternate daily patrols of Vitiaz Strait. Known within the unit as the Tuluvu Expeditionary Force, the detachment installed a runway lighting system with flare pots for evening patrols.

Throughout late November the No. 3 *Chutai* conducted night shipping patrols, many of which were foiled by bad weather. In the last days of the month four light bombers attacked US infantry positions north of Finschhafen, and despite return fire none of the attackers was hit. The Ki-51s continued to reconnoiter Allied troop positions around Finschhafen on late afternoon missions but found no targets. Up against a lack of spare parts, both the Tuluvu and Alexishafen Ki-51 detachments struggled to keep even a modest inventory airworthy.

Overall the unit achieved limited success, yet the Tuluvu Expeditionary Force was singled out for commendation by the commander of the 6th *Hikoshidan*, Lieutenant-General Itahana Gi'ichi, when he issued his farewell speech after being relieved of command for alleged failure to prevent the destruction of JAAF forces on the ground in New Guinea. The two *chutai* were nominally withdrawn from New Guinea to Hollandia in late January 1944 due to ongoing Allied air attack, however the reality is that by this stage most of their Ki-51s had been destroyed.

Chutai colors were blue for the No. 2 *Chutai* commanded by Lieutenant Yoshida Tateki, and yellow for the No. 3 *Chutai*. The tail motif is an artistic and composite horizontal interpretation of the *kanji* number 26 (二十六). This same motif also appeared on the unit's No. 1 *Chutai* Ki-43-II *Hayabusa* however this *chutai* never served in New Guinea. Sometimes the motif had narrow white piping applied to accentuate it from the camouflage background. All Ki-51 airframes left the factory painted overall in a light ash blue/green. Each aircraft was individually camouflaged in the field in differing shades of green, ranging from overall schemes to mottled and snake-weave applications, and sometimes a combination of the two.

A pair of No. 2 Chutai Ki-51s airborne over New Guinea in late 1943, the foremost being the subject of Profile 18.

A factory-fresh Ki-51 has its guns aligned in Japan. The aircraft appears in the Mitsubishi semi-gloss light ash blue/green. Unit markings and camouflage will be applied in New Guinea.

Another view of the subject of the Three-Way Profile as abandoned on But 'drome's coastline.

On the rare occasions the Ki-51 was encountered over New Guinea it was nearly always and erroneously identified as either a Zeke or an Oscar.

Three Way Profile (opposite)

Note the reconnaissance camera fixed to the upper starboard wing. This airworthy 26th Sentai Ki-51 was one of 21 abandoned or destroyed in the Wewak area as surveyed on 27 June 1945 by Flight Lieutenant L Green, an RAAF Air Technical Intelligence Unit inspector. Abandoned on the beach near But 'drome, the unusual camouflage scheme is a hybrid of overall coverage and weave. Note the elevators' miniature weave pattern, likely applied by a groundcrew member with time on his hands, and the red piping on the combat stripe.

Three-Way Profile

15

16

17

18

Profiles 15-18 (Ki-51 Sonia)

15. This No. 3 *Chutai* Ki-51 without tail insignia was abandoned at But airfield.

16. Ki-51 MN 956 assigned to the No. 3 *Chutai* was abandoned at But airfield.

17. Ki-51 MN 2278 of the No. 2 *Chutai* was captured at Alexishafen.

18. The insignia on this No. 2 *Chutai* example has white piping applied. The overall spray did not extend to the cowl area.

The subject of Profile 16 as abandoned near But airfield.

A factory fresh Sokei leaves the Kawasaki factory, showcasing the overall cream finish applied to the airframe, underpinning all camouflage schemes applied in the field.

A No. 1 Chutai Sokei destroyed on the ground.

CHAPTER 6
The 34th *Hiko Sentai*

The 34th *Sentai* was activated in October 1942 at Hokota, Japan, with Ki-48-I light bombers. In February 1943 the unit transferred to the French airfield at Pochentong, just outside Phnom Penh. In October 1943 it moved again to Burma, operating between there and Thailand depending on the seasons.

With most bomber units in New Guinea reduced to a handful of aircraft by the end of 1943, JAAF command decided to redeploy the 34th *Sentai* from Chieng Mai, Thailand, to Hollandia. Now operating upgraded Ki-48-II models and commanded by Lieutenant Colonel Tanaka Sukeharu, the unit spent nearly two weeks at Hollandia before detachments progressed to Hansa Bay and Dagua where they were maintained by 208th *Sentai* personnel, another *Sokei* unit. Then, in February 1944, 4th Air Army operations orders assigned Hansa Bay as an emergency landing field for 63rd and 248th *Sentai* fighters, along with the light bombers of the 34th and 208th *Sentai*.

Meanwhile the unit's approximately two hundred ground crew prepared to leave Chieng Mai while the aircrew, five crew per bomber instead of the usual four, flew their Ki-48-II *Sokei* to New Guinea via Bangkok, Singapore, Bandung, Malang, Makassar and Ceram before arriving at Hollandia on 19 February 1944. Fifteen *Sokei* made this initial journey, comprising seven No. 1 *Chutai* bombers with 35 flight personnel led by *chutaicho* Captain Okami Kinichi, and eight more assigned to No. 2 *Chutai* with 42 airborne personnel led by *chutaicho* Masui Yoshiro. The ground crew meanwhile were flown by transports to Manila. Their journey from here was interrupted and they never arrived at Hollandia due to Allied air attacks. Meanwhile on 23 February 1944, three more *Sokei* arrived to reinforce the No. 1 *Chutai*, plus another two to reinforce the No. 2 *Chutai*. A small Headquarters detachment stayed behind at Hollandia to conduct administrative and liaison duties.

At Hollandia the *sentai* was placed under the command of the Hakujoshi Operational Training *Hikodan*. It was planned that the bombers based at Dagua and Hansa Bay would support the 18th Army's operations with medium altitude missions. Each crew member carried two oxygen bottles to be used at altitudes above 4,000 metres (12,500 feet) for this purpose, however these detachments had barely deployed before they suffered substantive losses to ongoing and relentless USAAF air attacks. As such, the 34th *Sentai* in New Guinea conducted barely any combat missions. Those it flew were usually conducted in six-bomber formations due to the lack of aircraft.

During a low-level 12 April 1944 Hollandia attack, all of the unit's spare parts, oil and ammunition supplies were destroyed, along with five more *Sokei*. On 17 April the unit's five surviving bombers at Hollandia retreated to Wakde to remove themselves from more American air attacks. Those crew left behind were either captured, starved to death or over the next few months were killed fighting US soldiers. Although the unit was officially disbanded on 25 July

1944, it had in fact ceased to exist a few months prior, with its handful of surviving *Sokei* in New Guinea absorbed by the 208th *Sentai*.

Markings

All men serving the unit all wore an insignia on their uniform above the right breast pocket with the *kanji* characters 田仲 representing the surname (Tanaka) of their commander, with 田 being the predominantly large character. The unit's distinctive tail insignia derives from a stylised interpretation of the *kanji* characters for the numerals 3 and 4 (三 and 四), introduced shortly after the unit was formed at Hokota. All *Sokei* left the Kawasaki factory painted in overall light brown cream, and camouflage was applied in the field. A range of overall green schemes were carried forward from Indochina, mixed with other field-applied varieties. By the time the unit reached New Guinea most replacement bombers were given weave patterns which varied in style and intensity. *Chutai* colours were white, yellow and red for the Nos 1, 2 and 3 *Chutai*, with blue for the small headquarters detachment. No other discernible markings such as *kanji* names or painted rudder trim tabs are seen on the modest number of photos extant of this unit.

A pair of 34th Sentai Sokei photographed at Hollandia during one of the April 1944 low-level strikes, without tail insignia.

A close-up of the tail insignia of a No. 1 Chutai Sokei destroyed at Hollandia.

PACIFIC PROFILES

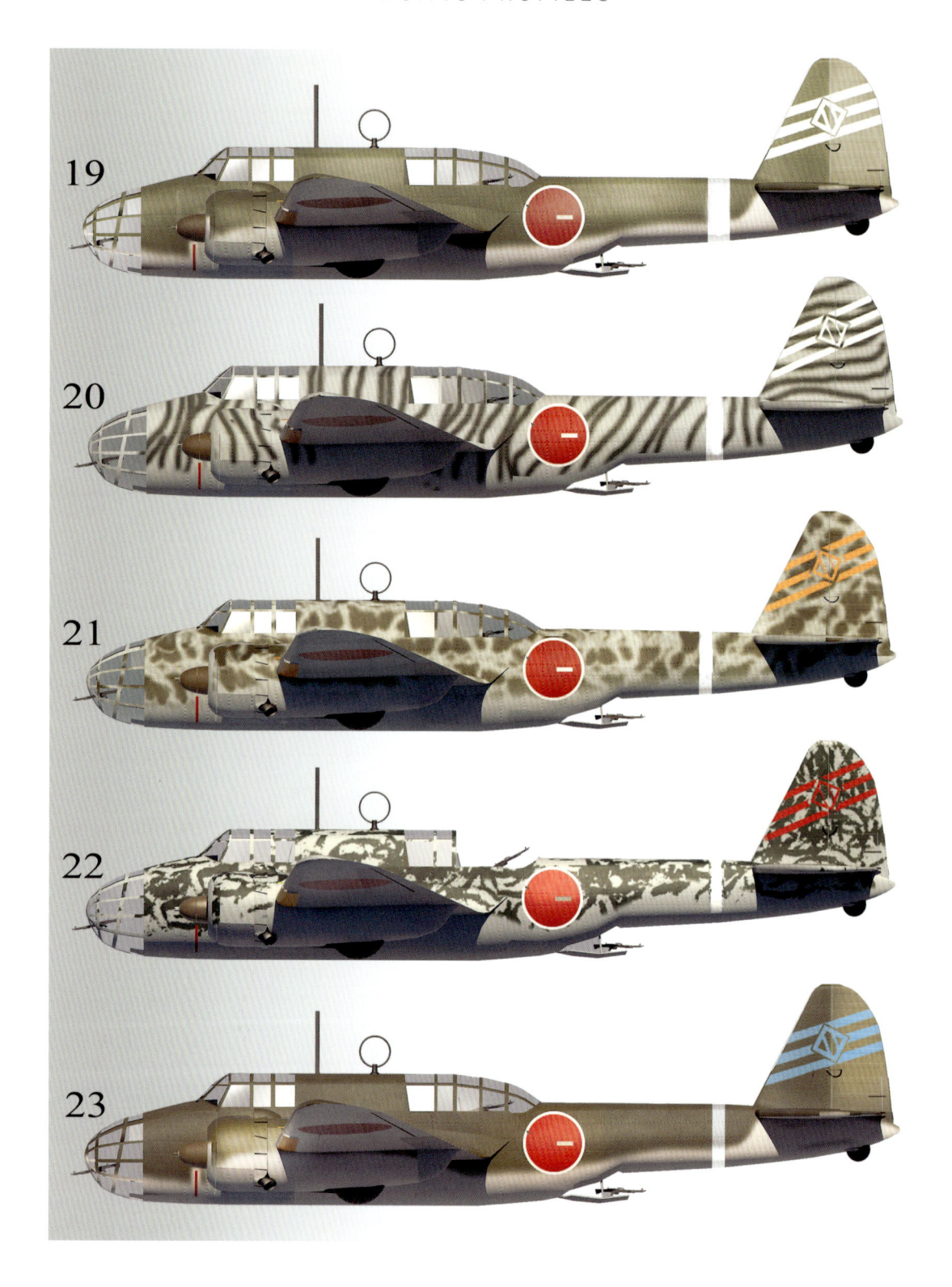

19

20

21

22

23

Profiles 19-23 (Ki-48 *Sokei* / Lily)

19. This No. 1 *Chutai* Ki-48-II was photographed over Thailand just prior to the New Guinea deployment and arrived at Hollandia on 19 February 1944.
20. This No. 1 *Chutai* Ki-48-II served at Hollandia in February 1944 and was destroyed on the ground at Wakde after evacuating New Guinea.
21. This No. 2 *Chutai* Ki-48-II served in New Guinea in late February 1944.
22. This No. 3 *Chutai* Ki-48-II with weave camouflage was destroyed on the ground during the March 1944 Hollandia strikes.
23. Ki-48-II assigned to the headquarters detachment at Hollandia. Another *Sokei* also with blue headquarters tail insignia was examined at Sawar in July 1944.

The No. 1 Chutai flies over Thailand jungle near the border town of Chieng Mai just prior to the New Guinea deployment in February 1944. This aircraft is subject of Profile 20.

The subject of Profile 24 at Munda being prepared for shipment to Australia for intelligence analysis.

The subject of Profile 26 as captured at Hollandia in April 1944, behind which is the wreckage of a 7th Sentai Donryu.

CHAPTER 7
The 45th *Hiko Sentai*

Behind the history of the 45th *Sentai*, the first JAAF light bomber unit to reach New Guinea, lies a curious antiquity. By the time the US declared war on Japan, an institutional Japanese mindset prevailed that the IJN flew solely over the sea while the JAAF restricted itself to land operations. This preconception was about to be challenged by the vast geography of the Pacific. The initial JAAF reluctance to commit air units to the Southeast Area derived from its judgement that over-water distances were best negotiated by the IJN. When the JAAF finally acquiesced to political pressure to deploy there, it well understood the reality that its aircrews had limited experience to deal with such challenges.

Both the 45th *Sentai*, commanded by Lieutenant Colonel Yasuoka Mitsuo with his deputy Major Takahashi Kenichi, and its sister unit the 208th *Sentai* fell under the command of the Hakujoshi Operational Training *Hikodan*. However, the "training" designation is deceptive. Both units were combat units, however the role of the Hakujoshi Flying School was to train aircrew for long distance navigation over featureless desert, a skill useful for negotiating vast oceanic distances. Hakujoshi was located on the central Manchuria plain, and was thus central to extensive and featureless geography. The JAAF thus chose these two bomber units for the initial Pacific deployment as they were the best qualified units for long distance navigation.

Both deployed a mixture of the latest Ki-48-II *Sokei* models which started leaving Kawasaki's factory shortly after the Pacific War commenced, complementing an inventory of earlier model Ki-48-Is which the 45th commenced operating on 1 September 1940, replacing its Ki-32s. The Ki-48-II had a longer and stronger fuselage than the Ki-48-I and more powerful engines with a two-stage blower, limited fuel tank protection and crew armour. The Ki-48-II-*otsu* was fitted with retractable dive brakes, which the 45th removed in the New Guinea theatre to save weight. Most New Guinea operations favoured low to medium altitude missions.

In December 1942 the 45th *Sentai* loaded twenty *Sokei* aboard the aircraft transport *Ryuho* which departed Yokosuka on 11 December 1942 bound for Truk. From there the bombers would be flown to Rabaul. However only one day into the voyage the *Ryuho* was hit by a torpedo forcing it to return to Japan for repairs. The *Sokei* were transferred to the aircraft carrier *Zuikaku* for successful delivery directly to Rabaul. They based themselves at Rapopo south of Rabaul and became the first unit to operate from the newly built airfield.

On 22 January 1943 the unit deployed to Munda Airfield in the Solomons to support Operation Ke, the evacuation of Guadalcanal, by bombing US troop positions. In fact, the unit only flew one mission there on 27 January in conjunction with *Hayabusa* from the 1st and 11th *Sentai*. Two days later all of the unit's bombers evacuated to Ballale overnight to avoid US bombing, however upon return to Munda the following day the unit lost five *Sokei* to Allied attacks. After this the 45th *Sentai* returned to Rapopo. Next, the deteriorating situation on the New Guinea mainland saw the 45th *Sentai* move to Lae to support Japanese attempts to capture Wau, in the mountains behind the town. On 6 February 1943 nine No. 3 *Chutai Sokei* headed off to bomb Wau, escorted by 29 Ki-43-I *Hayabusa* from the 11th *Sentai*. The unit lost three bombers during this attack, one claimed by AA fire and two more by USAAF fighters.

Few *Sokei* crewmembers survived their New Guinea deployment, exemplified by a lucky escape on 26 September 1943 when No. 1 *Chutai* pilot Noguchi Shigeyuki was chased by a trio of U.S fighters over Finschhafen. He escaped back to Wewak by retreating at full power just above the trees with his dorsal gunner barely deterring the pursuers. Noguchi's lucky survival highlights the *Sokei*'s only realistic defence: low-level retreat. New Guinea crews detested the *Sokei* nicknaming it *satsujinki* (suicide plane). Its failings included an ineffective bomb load, poor maneuverability and a slow rate of climb. The temperamental magnetos regularly faltered and sometimes completely failed.

Markings

Prior to arriving in the Pacific the 45th *Sentai* applied the *sakura* (cherry blossom) in the centre of the tails of its *Sokei*. Emblematic and philosophical, the *sakura* became a landmark symbol for Japan's identity in WWII, becoming a representation of hope to motivate the war effort. It was adopted by the government and imperial forces to unify the nation in its struggle, and often appeared in metaphors in motivational speeches. It was a common emblem in both JAAF and IJN insignia. The *chutai* colours were white, red, and yellow for the No. 1, 2 and 3 *Chutai*, defined in the colour of the respective *sakura*, with blue for the headquarters detachment.

When the unit first arrived in theatre, rudders often carried place names in hand-painted *hiragana* which also served as a call-sign, with the following names:

- Headquarters detachment: Shikishima, Takemitsu, Marukame and Kamachi.

- No. 1 *Chutai*: Biwako, Chichibu, Ayame, Kaede, Asashi, Kasuga, Shiranami, Kakori, Matsushima and Oshima.

- No. 2 *Chutai*: Nakano, Takasago, Kisokawa, Haneda, Take, Sensui, Mikawa and Fukushima.

- No. 3 *Chutai*: Wakagusa, Hamada, Abukuma, Yama, Tashima, Mikazuki, Karatachi, Kurogame and Ashigara.

Towards the end of the New Guinea tour it was decided that the *sakura* stood out too much, so they were painted over. Later, for *chutai* identification, the Roman numerals I, II or III were hand-painted on the fuselage in white to denote the respective *chutai*.

It is unclear why, even though both the 45th and 208th *Sentai* were combat units, they remained under a parent "training" *Hikodan*, often abbreviated to the Kyodo *Hikodan* throughout its deployment to New Guinea and the Solomons. This *Hikodan* was redesignated the 30th *Hikodan* in late March 1944 when the 45th *Sentai* was at Hollandia with a dozen remaining *Sokei* on charge. The unit was eventually disbanded in August 1944, after briefly re-equipping with the Ki-45 which it operated in West New Guinea.

Ki-48-Is from the No. 2 Chutai heading out from Rabaul during the unit's early deployment.

The forward half of a white sakura emblem with a blue stem on the tail of a Ki-48-I, captured at Munda, August 1943.

Another 45th Sentai Ki-48-II being loaded at Munda for intelligence analysis in Australia.

The fin of this 45th Sentai Ki-48 at Munda has produced several faulty speculative profiles over the years. Some artists have misinterpreted the wear on the metal as a kanji character. Photos of the fin from other angles demonstrate clearly it is paint wear from the tropics.

THE 45TH HIKO SENTAI

Abandoned at Dagua, MN 1371 is from the No. 2 Chutai as demonstrated by the Roman numerals II on the fuselage, hand-painted in white about halfway down the fuselage. The numerals 71 appear on the forward fuselage, and this bomber is the subject of Profile 28.

A white sakura seen on a Ki-48-II at Wewak during a low-level strike.

PACIFIC PROFILES

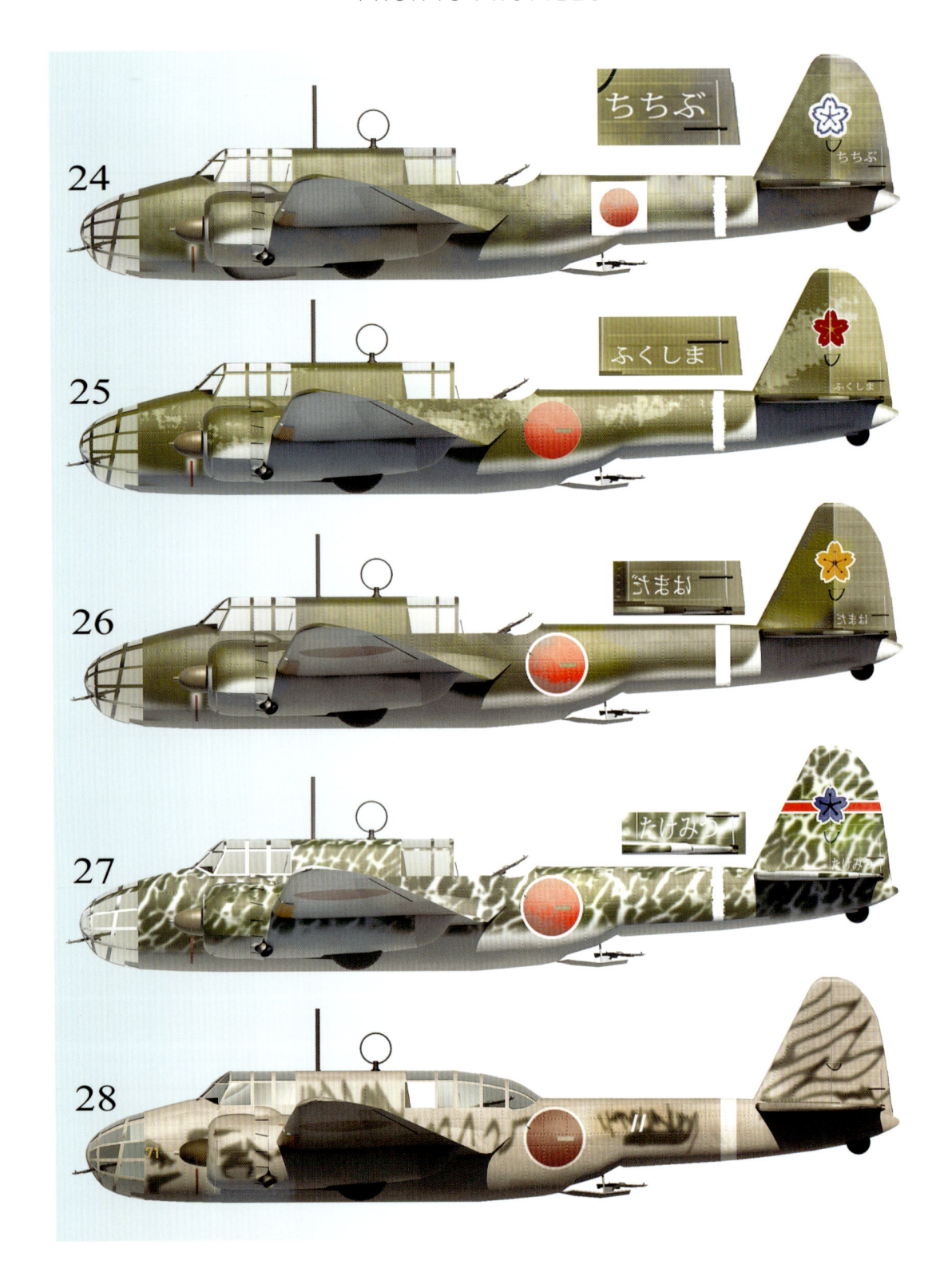

24

25

26

27

28

Profiles 24–28 (Ki-48 *Sokei* / Lily)

24. Ki-43-I MN 534 from the No. 1 *Chutai* was abandoned at Munda. It retained a white square around the *hinomaru*, left over from its training days in Manchuria. The profile has the *Hiragana* "Chichibu" (ちちぶ) on the rudder, one of the No. 1 *Chutai*'s names and call-signs.

25. This Ki-48-II from the No. 2 *Chutai* was abandoned at Hollandia. It has the *Hiragana* "Fukushima" (ふくしま) on the rudder, one of No. 2 *Chutai*'s names and call-signs.

26. This Ki-48-II from the No. 3 *Chutai* was abandoned at Wewak. It has the *Hiragana* "Hamada" (はまだ) on the rudder, one of the No. 3 *Chutai*'s names and call-signs.

27. This Ki-48-II from the headquarters detachment had an additional red bar across the fin to complement the blue *sakura*. It was assigned to the unit's commanding officer Lieutenant Colonel Yasuoka Mitsuo, and carried one of four names: either Shikishima, Takemitsu, Marukame or Kamachi. It was abandoned at Hollandia, and for illustration purposes appears with the name Takemitsu (たけみつ).

28. Towards the last phase of its New Guinea deployment the unit abandoned the *sakura* for camouflage purposes, and hand-painted in Roman numbers I, I or II on the side of the fuselage to denote the respective *chutai*. The white numerals II denote the No. 2 *Chutai* on this example, found abandoned at Dagua.

PACIFIC PROFILES

The subject of Profile 32 as abandoned at Wakde. (courtesy Darryl Ford)

The tail of the subject of Profile 29 as abandoned at Hollandia.

CHAPTER 8
The 60th *Hiko Sentai*

The 60th *Sentai* commanded by Major Oiwa Mitsuo was part of the 8th *Hikodan* when it advanced its Ki-21-IIs to New Guinea from Malang on Java in March 1944. It arrived late into the New Guinea air war where its combat role was limited. Wakde was designated as the forward operating base of the unit, however the unit's bombers were soon focused on ferrying supplies and personnel into the New Guinea theatre.

An advance contingent flew to Wakde Island on 10 March 1944, and thence started supply and evacuation missions to and from Hollandia and the Wewak area. Bombers from this unit now became involved in some of the last-minute attempts to rescue JAAF personnel from New Guinea airfields. On 13 March Allied air reconnaissance ascertained there were 47 aircraft on the ground at Wakde. A few days prior the 60th *Sentai* listed fifteen airworthy Ki-21 heavy bombers. That afternoon a single 60th *Sentai* Ki-21-II based at But 'drome claimed hits on a medium transport ship when attacking Hyane in the Admiralties, however the USN reported this attack as ineffective.

The unit lost several bombers to the USAAF raids on Hollandia from 29 to 31 March 1944, and six more at Wakde, leaving a total inventory of a dozen airworthy bombers. Although they retreated back to Wakde Island, Babo and Morotai, small flights continued to attempt rescue missions, the last of which was made on 21 April 1944 when two No. 3 *Chutai* Ki-21s attempted a rescue mission from Biak to Wewak. At Wewak they were to evacuate key officers to Manado in the Celebes, however both bombers flown by Lieutenants Gojima and Ueda (first names unknown) were shot down by USAAF fighters just before they reached Wewak.

Markings

Chutai colours were white, red and yellow for the Nos. 1, 2 and 3 *Chutai*, commanded by Captain Kono (first name unknown), Lieutenant Ogino Koji and Captain Sato (first name unknown) respectively. The unit insignia was a broad horizontal band across the tail. Many bombers were named, the only known example being Sano 佐野 a city located in Tochigi Prefecture. Some bombers also had a thin white oblique line incorporated across the insignia band. This might have been a *shotaicho* marking, however this is unconfirmed.

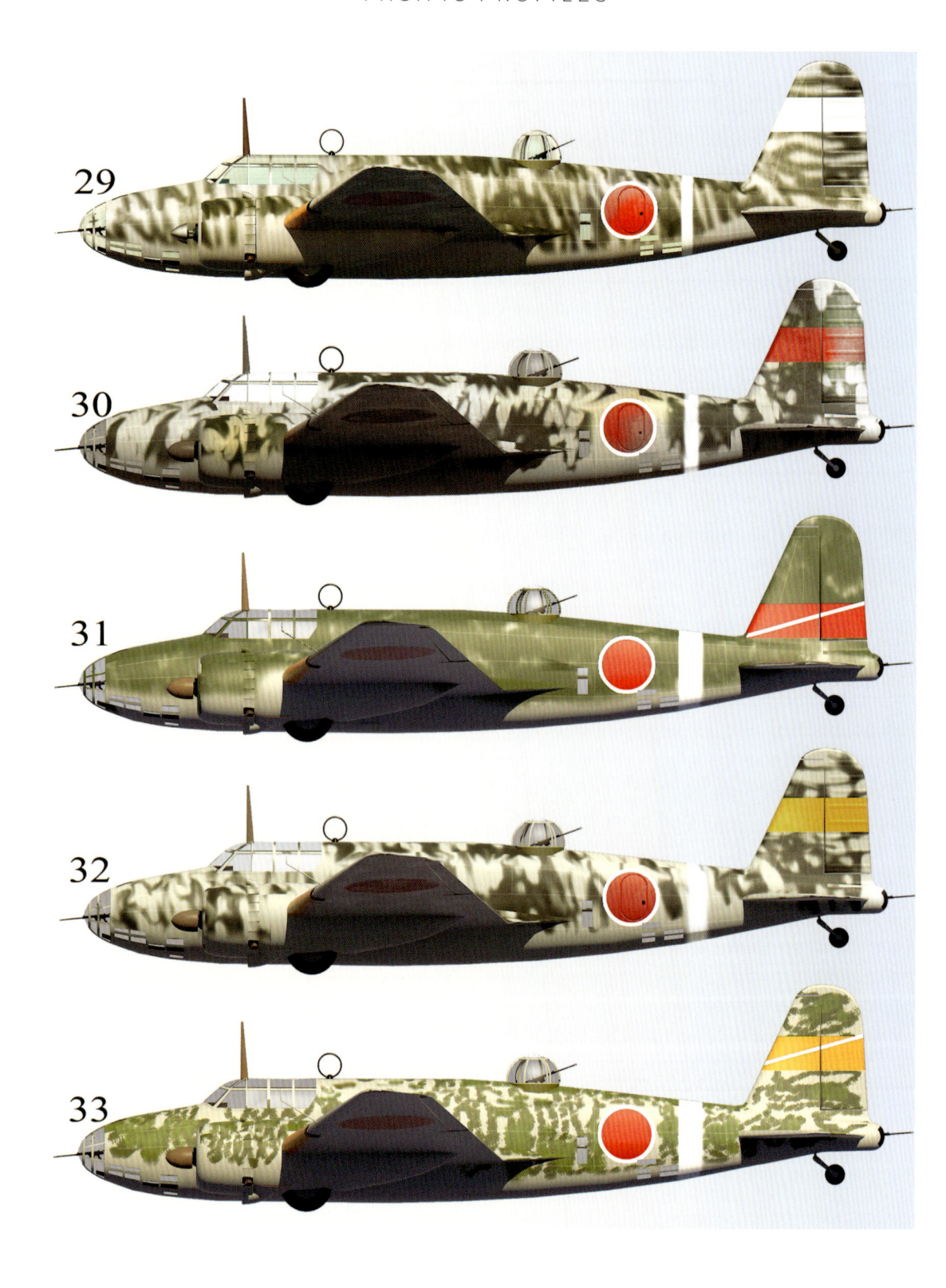

PACIFIC PROFILES

29

30

31

32

33

Profiles 29-33 (Ki-21 Sally)

29. Ki-21-II of the No. 1 *Chutai* abandoned at Hollandia, April 1944.
30. Ki-21-II of the No. 2 *Chutai* abandoned at Wakde.
31. Ki-21-II of the No. 2 *Chutai* photographed in late 1943. Note the fin stripe is positioned lower than normal.
32. Ki-21-II of the No. 3 *Chutai* abandoned at Wakde.
33. Ki-21-II of the No. 3 *Chutai* photographed in late 1943.

Another view of the subject of Profile 32 as abandoned at Wakde. (courtesy Darryl Ford)

An early model Ki-49-I Donryu seen on the ground at Rapopo in late 1943, visiting Rabaul during a transport run.

Hokoku 1249 patriotic donation Ki-49-II Donryu abandoned at Hollandia.

The early unit insignia is displayed on this Ki-49 found at Hollandia and the subject of Profile 36.

This late model Ki-49-II was captured at Wakde. (courtesy Darryl Ford)

CHAPTER 9
The 61st *Hiko Sentai*

The 61st *Sentai* commanded by Lieutenant Colonel Yagi Takeshi was assigned to the 9th *Hikodan* and was the first unit to operate the Nakajima *Donryu* heavy bomber in the JAAF. While converting to the Ki-49-I from the Ki-21 at Hamamatsu training base in June 1943, the unit was ordered to deploy to Timor from where it conducted three missions over Australian targets. Two *Donryu* were lost on a combat mission over Darwin on 20 June, with the two commanders being No.1 *Chutai chutaicho* Captain Ota Katsuhiro and Lieutenant Matubara Kenjiro.

When redeployed to the New Guinea theatre, the unit first sent an advance detachment to But airfield from where on 6 September 1943 it flew its first mission in New Guinea. The following month the unit minus the No. 2 *Chutai* moved its headquarters to Wakde, where it was joined by Ki-21 transports of the 101st Air Transport Unit. Throughout October and November, it struggled to keep half a dozen bombers operational at Wakde.

When the 61st *Sentai* arrived at But it often paired with the 7th *Sentai* for combat missions. It flew most of its combat missions from But airfield, however both heavy bomber units often found themselves assigned to conducting supply operations in support of beleaguered 18th Army troops between Finschhafen and Sio on New Guinea's north coast. The unit's main combat target was the growing Allied air bases in the Markham and Ramu Valleys including the expanding USAAF Nadzab air base. Then, in December 1943 when US troops landed at Arawe and Cape Gloucester on New Britain, its bombers suffered badly during attacks mounted against these landings. For a time in late 1943, the 7th *Sentai* was withdrawn from combat leaving the weakened 61st *Sentai* as the JAAF's sole heavy bomber unit in New Guinea.

Planners back in Japan had earlier earmarked Port Moresby as a priority target for the Ki-49s, in order to demonstrate a JAAF long-range offensive capacity. However, Ki-49s only got there once, on 20 September 1943. During this mission four bombers launched from Dagua airfield in late evening heavy rain, however stormy conditions soon forced two to turn back, one of which ditched off Wewak drowning all of the crew. Two Ki-49s flown by Jushiro Ikejima and Toyo'o Sakura got through to bomb Port Moresby's airfields, but rendered only slight damage. It was the final Japanese air-raid against the town for the entire war. The mission was also the final offensive one for the *Donryu* in New Guinea.

By mid-January 1944 reinforcements briefly brought the 61st *Sentai* up to strength with fifteen serviceable bombers. Further reinforcements would soon substantially increase the number of aircraft at Wakde, however these were soon destroyed by US air raids. On 3 March 1944 P-38 ace Richard Bong and Thomas Lynch engaged JAAF fighters and bombers, and one of those shot down was a *Donryu* commanded by Lieutenant Sakai Kazuo. On 13 March the 61st *Sentai* listed only five operational *Donryu*. Then, on 16 March the unit lost one in an accident, underlining its centre-of-gravity problems experienced during take-offs. Warrant Officer Minami Keizo and crew were killed when they scrambled after an air-raid warning. The bomber turned too sharply on take-off and stalled before coming down in a coconut plantation. During the month of March, the unit sometimes dispersed its fleet from Wakde to Kamiri to guard against possible air attack. Throughout early 1944 the unit also ran numerous liaison and mail runs throughout the region on behalf of the 4th Air Army.

Markings

Most *Donryu* were camouflaged in overall green at Hamamatsu training base before deployment to Timor. These early model Ki-49-Is applied an oblique forward-slanting stripe across the fin (see Profile 36), in *chutai* colours of yellow, blue and red for the Nos. 1, 2 and 3 *Chutai* respectively. Some of these made their way to New Guinea, however the majority deployed to New Guinea were Ki-49-IIs which were applied with a variety of weave and blotch camouflage patterns. The oblique stripe insignia was abandoned in New Guinea as it was judged too obvious a marking for Allied fighters to see. Instead, *Donryu* arriving in theatre had a variety of camouflage schemes, with some having their name / call-sign hand-painted on the rudder as illustrated in Profile 38.

Profiles 34-38 (Ki-49 Donryu / Helen)

34. Ki-49-II MN 3297 crashed at Cape Gloucester in late 1943. The bomber sports a splotch camouflage.

35. This late model Ki-49-II was abandoned Hollandia April 1944. It is *hokoku* patriotic donor aircraft 愛国1423 (廣島電氣) "Patriotic Donation 1423 (Hiroshima Electrical Company)", donated on 23 August 1943.

36. Operated by the No. 3 *Chutai*, this is a Ki-49-I which carried the early oblique tail marking and overall green camouflage. This aircraft was abandoned at Hollandia where the aircraft had been primarily used as a transport.

37. This late model Ki-49-II was captured at But, and carries a striking "zebra" camouflage scheme, common to many of the unit's late model Ki-49-IIs.

38 Ki-49-II named and hand-painted with the *kanji* characters "Arakawa" 荒川 on the rudder. This *Donryu* operated from But in January 1944.

THE 61ST HIKO SENTAI

34

35
愛国-1423(廣島電氣)

36

37

38
荒川

The subject of Profile 42 is seen during a low-level strike against Hollandia in April 1944, with camouflage nets partly draped over the airframe.

The bomb mission symbols which appeared on the side of Profile 41, which was photographed at Hollandia after it was captured.

CHAPTER 10
The 75th *Hiko Sentai*

The 75th *Sentai* arrived at Hollandia in March 1944 from the Southwest theatre, where it had been involved in operations around the Netherlands East Indies (NEI). Its time in the New Guinea theatre was brief, during which it staged several missions through Alexishafen (Danip airfield).

The unit had ventured over Australia on 20 June 1943, when nine 75th *Sentai Sokei* were included in the first JAAF attack against Darwin. The raid was well executed with coordinated low and high-altitude attacks. Flying at high-altitude eighteen 61st *Sentai* Ki-49 *Donryu* escorted by 22 59th *Sentai Hayabusa* were engaged by RAAF Spitfires, while below them the nine *Sokei* dropped their bombs with impunity and made a low-level dash back to Timor. Two *Sokei* sustained damage from ground fire. Three months later the *Sokei* staged their second and last appearance over Australia in force. At mid-morning on 27 September 1943 21 *Sokei* bombed the airfield near Drysdale Mission in Western Australia, an ordnance depot for RAAF anti-submarine operations.

The unit took with it several early model Ki-48-Is to New Guinea which were remnants of the earlier NEI operations. In the face of relentless Allied bombing and strafing, in early April 1944 it was decided to withdraw the unit's remaining sixteen *Sokei* to the Philippines. In October 1944 it was pulled back to Japan to replenish.

Markings

Unit markings have been misrepresented over the years. This was largely due to assumptions by authors that the pre-war 1941 and then 1942 markings were carried into the NEI and New Guinea theatres. A stylised tail insignia combining the English numbers 7 and 5 is sometimes portrayed on the unit's bombers, however this was used after it left the New Guinea theatre. All technical reports, photos and post-war wreck surveys pertaining to New Guinea show use of the colours white, red and yellow for the Nos. 1, 2 and 3 *Chutai* respectively. It is possible that the headquarters detachment used blue, however no proof has surfaced to date.

Unit insignia was a wide band applied about two-thirds up the tail, on which usually appeared a name. This was a practice which commenced before the unit's deployment to New Guinea and showcased the names of geographic features in Japan (especially mountains). Later these were substituted for the surnames of famous personalities, depending on *chutai* preference. These were hand-written in *hiragana* over the band on the fin in either white or black, depending on the colour of the band. These names were also used as call-signs for communications purposes.

Known names / call-signs include Izu いづ (named after the Izu Peninsula and also carried on a pre-war *Sokei*), Asama あさま (a mountain in Honshu), Minimi みなみ (an unknown name association seen at Hollandia), Tokiwa ときわ (a town near Mount Fuji), and Akagi (a mountain in Gunma prefecture).

Curiously, the only known example of JAAF bombing mission markings appearing in the theatre appeared on the fuselage of a 75th *Sentai Sokei* destroyed at Hollandia, as illustrated in Profile 41.

As USAAF "parafrags" float down, a No. 3 Chutai Sokei is photographed at an unknown New Guinea location in early April 1944. This bomber has an overall green application, indicating the likelihood it is an earlier Ki-48-I brought from the NEI theatre.

Profiles 39-42 (Ki-48 *Sokei* / Lily)

39. Ki-48-II assigned to the No. 2 *Chutai*, callsign Izu いづ.

40. Ki-48-II assigned to the No. 1 *Chutai*, callsign Asama あさま and surveyed by ATIU at Hollandia.

41. Ki-48-II abandoned at Hollandia from an unknown *chutai*, with bomb mission symbols painted in red on the fuselage.

42. Ki-48-II assigned to the No. 2 *Chutai*, call-sign Minimi (みなみ), which was photographed at Hollandia.

43. Ki-48-I MN 484 assigned to the No. 3 *Chutai*. This aircraft crashed in a gully approaching Alexishafen airfield (Danip), on an unknown date. A post-war survey found evidence of a yellow fin band. The name Tokiwa ときわ has been applied for illustrative purposes only – it is not necessarily associated with this airframe.

THE 75TH HIKO SENTAI

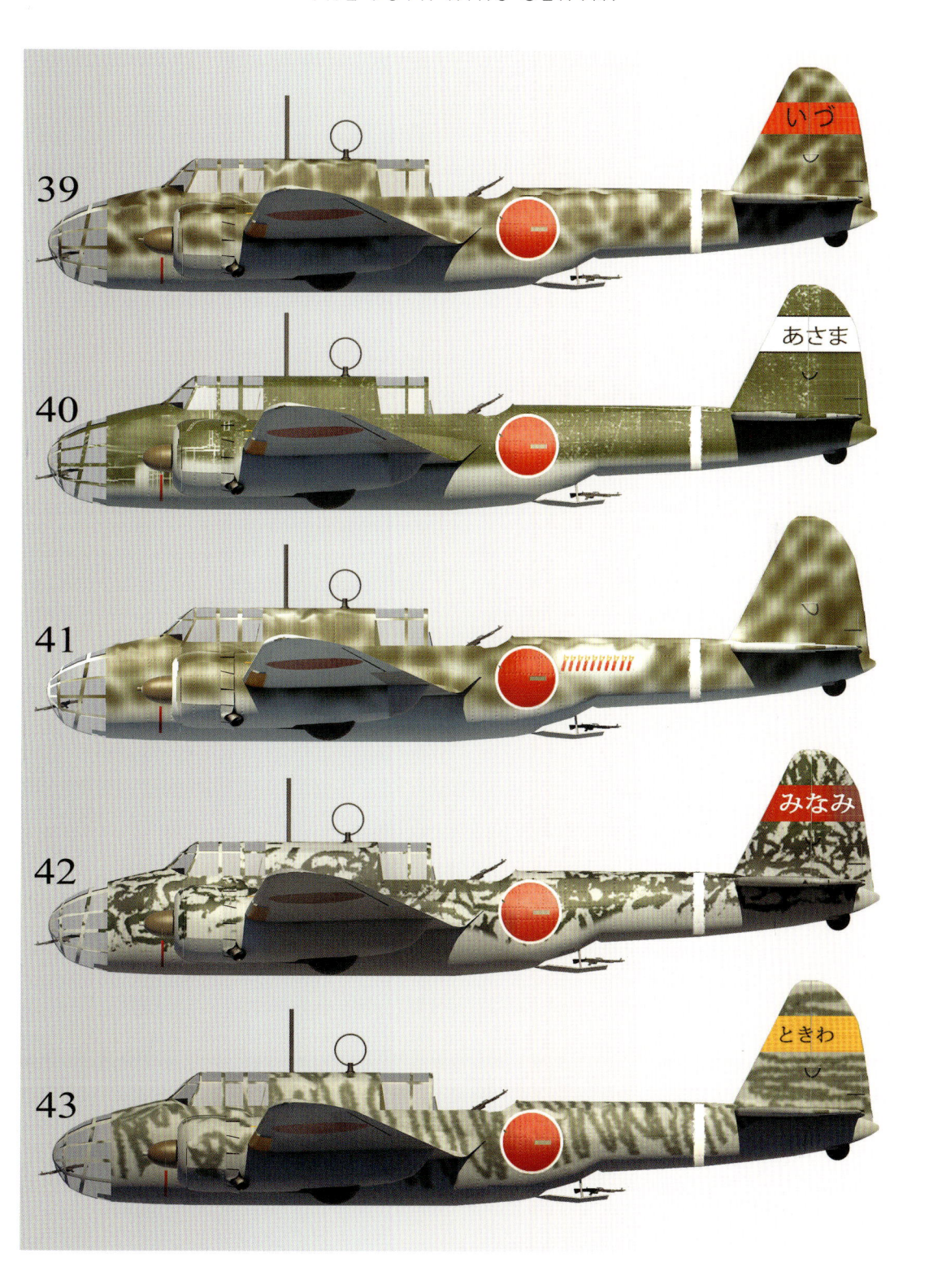

39

40

41

42

43

The subject of Profile 45 captured at Lae.

A No. 3 Chutai Ki-48-II as evidenced by the yellow trim tab, seen at Hollandia during a low-level strike just prior to the invasion.

The subject of Profile 48 in long grass at Dagua.

CHAPTER 11
The 208th *Hiko Sentai*

Both the 208th *Sentai* and its sister unit the 45th *Sentai* fell under the command of the Hakujoshi Operational Training *Hikodan*, however, as explained in Chapter 7, the "training" designation is deceptive. These two units were the most qualified in the JAAF for long distance navigation, and thus deemed as suitable for the challenges of oceanic Pacific navigation.

On 20 December 1942 as part of Operation Hinoe-Go 2, which was the reinforcement of New Guinea, the seaplane tender *Kiyokawa Maru* sailed from Yokosuka to Wewak to deliver spares and other supplies for the unit, along with ground personnel. The bulk of the regiment, including aircraft and aircrews, was later shipped from Yokosuka on the aircraft transporter *Chuyo*, and arrived in Truk on 12 February 1943. The *Sokei* were prepared for the voyage by draining fuel and sump oil, greasing propellers and undercarriages, and covering cockpit and cowling areas with tarpaulin. Wings were secured to the deck through wing tie-down bolts and the tail wheel. Brakes were set and tyre pressures were dropped for deck stability. At Truk the unit's 45 Ki-48-II *Sokei* were unloaded by barge and re-assembled.

On 3 May 1943 the entire regiment commanded by Lieutenant Colonel Oda Akimitsu attempted a long over-water delivery flight to reach Rabaul. Escorted by a *chutai* of IJN Zeros, frontal weather forced the return of the formation. One *Sokei* was destroyed on the return landing, and two Zeros collided head-on on the airfield, with another missing in the weather front. The regiment sat out nearly a week at Truk waiting for the weather to clear. A second delivery attempt was made on 9 May 1943, and all *Sokei* arrived safely at Vunakanau that afternoon. Two days later they flew the last leg to their new home of But airfield. Each *chutai* there built its own briefing shack using local materials. Equipped with rudimentary blackboards and maps, the shacks were located close to the field so aircraft movements could be monitored. The regiment arrived at But with only 44 pilots - one pilot per aircraft - however almost at once this critical resource was seriously challenged by malaria.

The unit's first combat mission in New Guinea proceeded on 15 May 1943. That afternoon, escorted by 11th *Sentai Hayabusa*, the *Sokei* attempted to bomb Australian positions at Bobdubi near Salamaua but instead accidentally bombed Japanese positions, killing and wounding 48 IJA soldiers. As the Japanese were still consolidating and expanding their hold around the Wewak area, local liaison missions took precedence for the next few weeks. Up to six passengers could be carried for such tasks. For example, on 18 May 1943, the No. 3 *Chutai chutaicho* took the CO of the 41st Division on a survey flight to ascertain the best place to build a bridge across the Sepik River. From 6 to 10 June the unit flew several missions to drop supplies to soldiers building a road from Wewak to Ambunti, about 70 miles inland from Wewak.

On 2 June 1943 sixteen *Sokei* escorted by 24th *Sentai Hayabusa* attacked Bulldog airfield to the northwest of Port Moresby. This was a long and challenging navigational flight of over four hundred miles, crossing the Owen Stanley Mountains. A RAAF transport was badly damaged, and two Australian soldiers were wounded as were three local labourers. Frightened by the bombs, hundreds of other labourers working on the airfield fled in fright, disrupting construction and maintenance work. One *Sokei* flown by Lieutenant Ezaki failed to return in the poor weather.

On 14 June 1943 seven *Sokei* from the No. 3 *Chutai* escorted by *Hayabusa* bombed the Australian outpost in the highlands at Kainantu, on another challenging flight of 250 miles with unfamiliar landmarks. On 20 June 1943 the unit returned to the Salamaua area to bomb Australian positions. One *Sokei* was slightly damaged over the target and overnighted at the new Japanese airfield at Hansa Bay. Later, from August 1943 onwards, the two Hansa Bay airfields (Awar and Nubia) were designated as forward operating bases for both the 45th and 208th *Sentai*. In November 1943 the entire unit briefly based itself at Awar. Meanwhile, among other surmounting problems, disease continued to significantly affect aircrew health and morale.

On 21 July 1943 a substantive fighter formation of 37 fighters, including eighteen recently arrived *Hien*, escorted eight *Sokei* to again attack Australian positions near Salamaua. About halfway back on the return track they encountered two squadrons of Lightnings near Bogadjim which fought the Japanese fighters. These successfully kept the Americans away from the *Sokei*, and although two Lightnings were lost, four *Hien* were shot down in return. On 15 August 1943, seven *Sokei* led by *chutaicho* Lieutenant Imai Hidezo were escorted mid-morning by 22 *Hayabusa* from the 59th *Sentai* and a dozen from the 24th *Sentai*, all led by Captain Nango Shigeo. The *Sokei* were attacked as they approached the target, the new American airfield being built at Tsili Tsili (termed Fabua by the Japanese). The Americans lost two transports and four fighters, while the Japanese lost three *Hayabusa* and six *Sokei*.

The American low-level strafing attacks against Wewak from 17 August 1943 destroyed many of the unit's aircraft, and as a result the unit was unable to mount any operations for the next two months. Increasing fuel shortages saw priority being given to fighters, and only a scarce number of replacement bombers arrived in November 1943. These were collected from Manila by the unit's pilots who were delivered there by air transport to collect them. Lieutenant Colonel Oda Akimitsu was replaced as CO by Major Tanaka Shozo in early October 1943 when Oda was recalled to a flying school position in Japan.

With serviceable bombers at a premium, late in the afternoon of 5 March 1944 American fighters shot down a *shotai* of three 208th *Sentai Sokei* flying in a "V" formation on a return leg to But Airfield. The *Sokei* dived westwards to try and escape by following the north coast just before all were quickly shot down. Nonetheless, having survived many Allied bombings the unit found sufficient resources on 15 March 1944 to launch five *Sokei* against Nadzab airfield. The five split into three groups, however marginal weather interfered, and the outcome of this mission is indicative of the odds such units faced in the New Guinea theatre. The first flight of two skirted the coast past Hansa Bay but could find no path through the rain. They wound up over Long Island before returning to Wewak. The second detachment led by Lieutenant Saito with Sergeant-Major Tsukagoe diverted to Dumpu where they dropped eight bombs. One of these two *Sokei* was shot down by anti-aircraft fire and crashed near Dumpu, while the final solitary bomber reached the coast near Manam Island but was also forced back by the weather. This typical futile mission resulted in negligible damage.

The unit had started evacuating its men to Hollandia in late March 1944, leaving about one hundred ground crew behind to fend for themselves. On the evening of 29 March fifteen of the unit's *Sokei* were destroyed by USAAF heavy bombers. On 19 April the unit's last remaining ten serviceable *Sokei* evacuated to Manila taking all remaining 30 pilots and a few hand-picked maintenance officers. During its one year in New Guinea, from May 1943 to April 1944, the 208th *Sentai* lost about 230 bombers: about 50 were lost in combat, about 100 were due to other operational and weather-related losses, and about 80 were lost in Allied air raids.

Markings

The last two digits of each manufacturer's number was painted on the tailfin. The No. 1 *Chutai* painted squared Arabic numerals in white, whilst the Nos. 2 and 3 *Chutai* had ordinary figures in white and yellow respectively. The colourful 208th *Sentai* insignia, a motif resembling the numbers two zeros and an eight, originally appeared on the unit's bombers in China but was painted over in New Guinea for security reasons. It was later reapplied when the unit withdrew to the Philippines. *Chutai* colours were white, red and yellow, and these were applied to the rudder trim tab.

The subject of Profile 46 is in the top left-hand corner, while MN 1377 is closest to the camera. The third aircraft is a Ki-57 transport, possibly assigned to the 11th Transport Detachment.

PACIFIC PROFILES

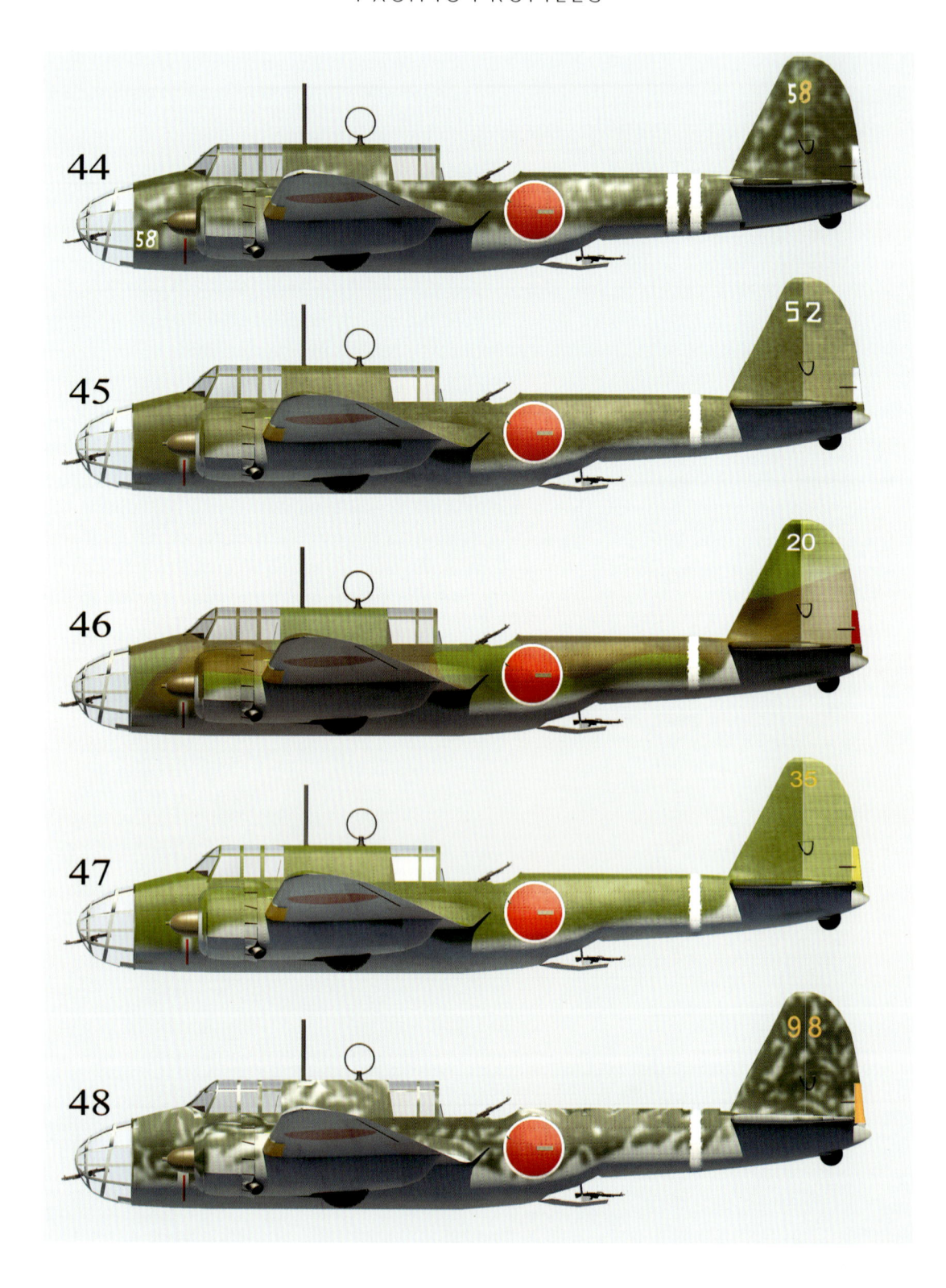

44

45

46

47

48

Profiles 44-48 (Ki-48 *Sokei* / Lily)

44. Ki-48-II MN 1258, the double white bands denote the No. 1 *Chutai chutaicho*. It was abandoned at Nubia, Hansa Bay.

45. Ki-48-II MN 1252 of the No. 1 *Chutai*, which was abandoned at Lae.

46. Ki-48-II MN 1120 of the No. 2 *Chutai*, which was abandoned at Hollandia.

47. Ki-48-II MN 1135 of the No. 3 *Chutai*, which was shot down near Tsili Tsili on 15 August 1943.

48. Ki-48-II MN 1398, of the No. 3 *Chutai* which was abandoned at Dagua.

Australian soldiers pose with the subject of Profile 44 at Nubia.

The subject of Profile 44 in full perspective, a chutaicho aircraft at Nubia.

PACIFIC PROFILES

This 6th Hikoshidan Ki-51 at Hollandia is the subject of Profile 56.

This 6th Hikoshidan Ki-51 at Hollandia is the subject of Profile 57.

CHAPTER 14
Headquarters and Command Units

Despite a theoretical rigid order-of-battle and command structure, JAAF deployment could be flexible under duress. Especially in the New Guinea theatre it proved it was able to improvise through necessity to try and surmount logistical gaps, especially those caused through unexpected system weaknesses imposed by combat.

Higher headquarters' detachments at *Hikodan* and *Hikoshidan* level were limited to around the size of a *shotai*, usually comprising the commander's aircraft, attended by an extra one or two transports, perhaps bolstered by several liaison aircraft. The mix thus usually included Ki-21s, Ki-57s or Ki-49s, and for short-range purposes Ki-51s or even *Hayabusa* served the purpose. Other command structures incorporated transport aircraft to ferry essential ground personnel. Sometimes an operational *hentai* of around eight pilots was assigned from the HQ detachment of the Army Air Transport Department (*Rikugun Koku Yuso*) directly to *Hikodan*-level. Their job was to fly or ferry reserve aircraft, and sometimes the *hentai* was briefly allocated under the command of those units being moved. Such assignments could be at short notice, especially if activated by shortfalls created by combat.

Whilst the *Hikodan* served primarily as an administrative organisation, aircraft and detached crews from other units could be assigned to *Hikodan*, pending permanent reallocation. Aircraft assigned to the three higher command levels, i.e. Air Force (*Kokugun*), Flying Division (*Hikoshidan*) or Flying Brigade (*Hikodan*), were based at airfields where the headquarters were based. In the New Guinea theatre these locations were Rabaul, Wewak or Hollandia.

Many aircraft were named via hand-painted *kanji* on either the nose or rudder of the aircraft. These names also served as call-signs, in varying sizes and calligraphy depending on the whim of the artist. Named 4th Air Army headquarters aircraft recorded by Allied intelligence include (with a flying hand motif) Nakagawa, Fukumiya, Jingo 神宮, Uyeda (assigned to a Ki-57), Liyeda and Yoshizawa. Those assigned to the 6th *Hikoshidan* include Makida (assigned to a Ki-21), Yokota 横田 (assigned to a Ki-51), Morori (assigned to a Ki-21) and Yokoyama (assigned to a Ki-21).

PACIFIC PROFILES

49

50

51

52

53

PAGE 76

4ᵗʰ Air Army Profiles 49–52

49. Ki-46-II MN 2485 forced-landed near Kimbe, New Britain, in early 1944. It was one of two of the type operated by the 4ᵗʰ Air Army HQ detachment in early 1944. The tail markings were red.

50. Ki-46-II MN 2406 was originally assigned to HQ of the 4ᵗʰ Air Army in mid-1943. It was later reassigned to the 74ᵗʰ Independent *Chutai* and crashed near But airfield (see Profile 66). This highly stylised white insignia was overpainted by the 74ᵗʰ's yellow river marking, as evidenced post-war through examination of the wreck.

51. This Ki-43-II was briefly used by 4ᵗʰ Air Army Headquarters before being reassigned to the 24th *Sentai*. It was captured at Hollandia. This aircraft appears in its later 24ᵗʰ *Sentai* marking as Profile 26 in *Pacific Profiles Volume One*.

52. This Ki-51 was captured at But 'drome with the 4ᵗʰ Air Army insignia hand-painted in white.

This 4ᵗʰ Air Army Ki-46 which force-landed in a swamp near Cape Gloucester airfield is the subject of Profile 49.

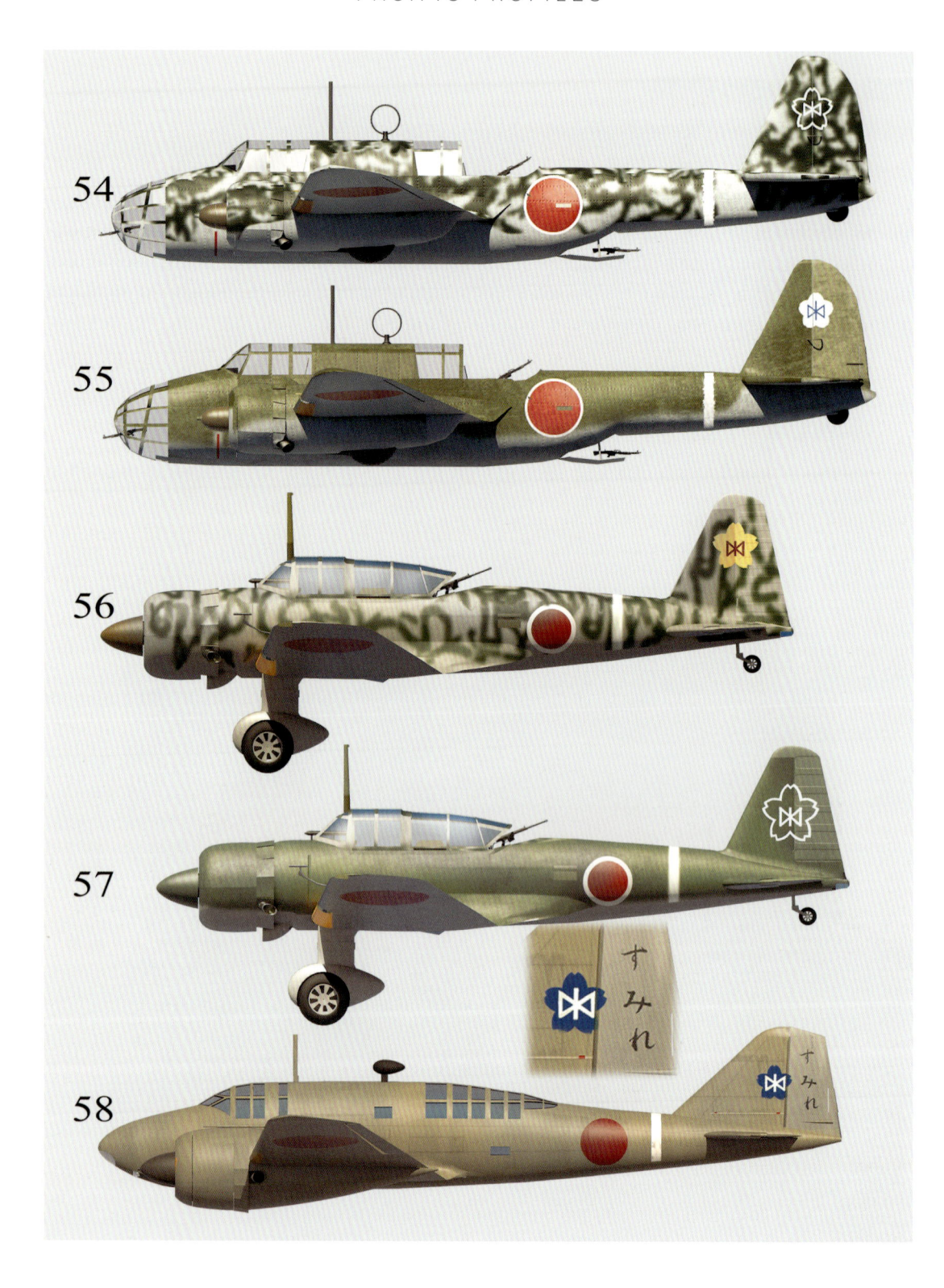

PACIFIC PROFILES

54

55

56

57

58

6th *Hikoshidan* Profiles 53-58

The JAAF used a series of signs for military usage which denoted different aircraft roles. The 6th *Hikodan* incorporated the triangle shape common to all its insignia, surrounded by a *sakura* (cherry blossom). While also used by the 45th *Sentai*, the emblematic *sakura* was a landmark symbol for Japan's identity in WWII and was used sparingly in JAAF insignia. The motif sometimes appeared with solid coloured backgrounds or stood by itself as a white shape. The meaning of the different colours and their variants is unclear, however they relate to the different purpose of each aircraft within the command structure, such as liaison, communications or VIP transport.

53. (Page 76) This Ki-21-II was destroyed on the ground at Hollandia.

54. This Ki-48-II *Sokei* was abandoned at Hollandia.

55. Two separate examples of the blue-on-white *sakura* were examined by Allied intelligence on Ki-48-IIs at Alexishafen and Madang.

56. This Ki-51 was abandoned in excellent condition at Hollandia.

57. This was another 6th *Hikoshidan* Ki-51 abandoned in excellent condition at Hollandia.

58. Ki-46-II MN 2251 named "Sumire" すみれ was captured at Lae in September 1943. The name refers to a violet species which is ubiquitous in Japan. It is also a female first name.

This 6th Hikoshidan Ki-51 at Hollandia is the subject of Profile 56.

PACIFIC PROFILES

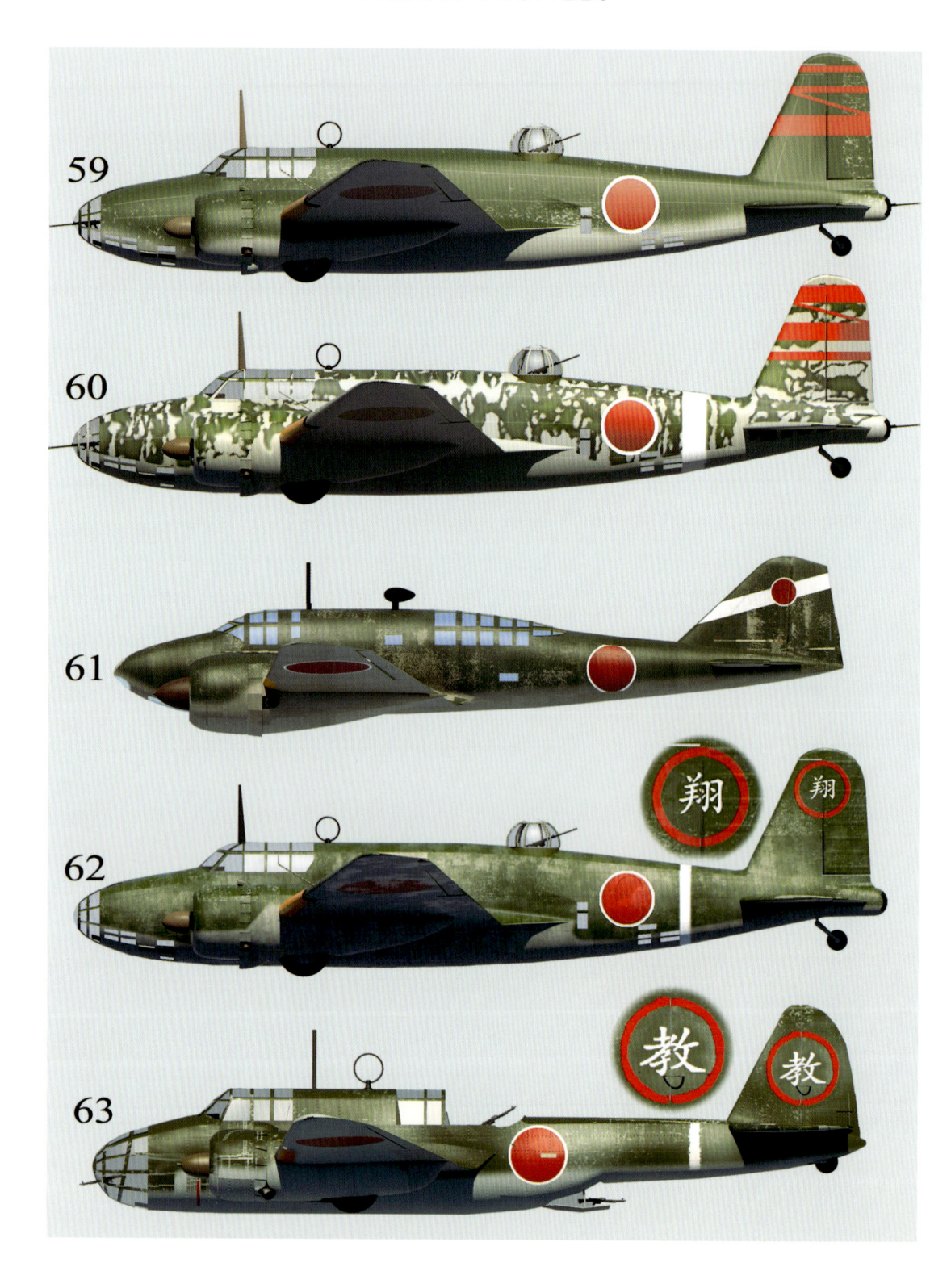

59

60

61

62

63

7th *Hikoshidan* and other Command Profiles

59. This Ki-21-II showcases the official guidelines for 7th *Hikoshidan* markings.

60. Post-war photos of Ki-21-II MN 4403 taken at Alexishafen have command markings which differ from the official guidelines as demonstrated in Profile 59 above. It appears the artist confused the order of narrow and broad bands when applying the markings.

61. This Ki-46-II was assigned to Air Army Headquarters in Tokyo and was destroyed by Allied bombing at Hollandia.

62. This Ki-21-II operated from Hollandia in February 1944 assigned to the 9th *Hikodan*. It carries the *kanji* character "sho" (翔 meaning "flying"), and was used by the commander and his staff.

63. This Ki-48-II was seen at But 'drome in December 1943 and on its fin is the *kanji* character "kyo" 教 an abbreviation of Kyodo 教道. The Kyodo *Hikodan* 教道飛行団 was a divisional flight school which originated in Hakujoshi 白城子 and was parent unit to both the 45th and 208th *Sentai*.

The circled tail of this Ki-46 at Hollandia denotes assignment to Air Army Headquarters in Tokyo and is the subject of Profile 61.

The tailplane of Profile 72. The 81st Dokuritsu Chutai was the only reconnaissance unit in New Guinea known to paint its horizontal stabilisers.

The common Mitsubishi light grey as applied to all Mitsubishi Ki-46-IIs is displayed on this captured example in the Philippines. (courtesy Darryl Ford)

Ground crew push a Ki-46-II from an unidentified reconnaissance unit under a camouflage net at But 'drome sometime in 1943.

CHAPTER 13
Reconnaissance Units

A mixture of JAAF reconnaissance units operated throughout the South Pacific, the majority of which were *Dokuritsu Chutai* (independent *chutai*) which answered directly to their parent *Hikodan*. Several were restructured during the New Guinea era, and aircraft were sometimes reassigned between units.

Both the Mitsubishi Ki-46 and Ki-51 were used for reconnaissance purposes, the former being used exclusively for long-range missions, including liaison, surveillance and photography. Many Ki-46 missions in New Guinea involved maritime patrols or searching for enemy aircraft. Ports and airfields were also priorities, the most important of which were photographed regularly. Patrols of four to five hours duration at up to 30,000 feet were commonplace, each covering different areas flown once every day. These missions always carried two crew, the pilot and observer who manned the radio and camera equipment. The Ki-46s were usually unarmed. Allied opposition presented only a limited threat. Flak was considered ineffective beyond 20,000 feet, and Allied fighters were rarely able to reach the Ki-46s at high altitude. Weather forecasts were obtained at Rabaul from the IJN and sometimes from Truk. Forecast winds were usually accurate, and navigation was conducted using dead reckoning. Radio silence was usually observed, and although a drift sight was installed in the Ki-46 they were rarely used.

Formation of the 70th, 74th and 76th *Dokuritsu Chutai*

These three reconnaissance units derived from a breakup of the pre-war 10th *Sentai* originally formed in August 1938 (not to be confused with the 10th *Dokuritsu Hikotai*, a separate JAAF unit). On 28 July 1941 the 10th *Sentai* was split into constituent independent squadrons whereby the No. 1 *Chutai* became the 70th *Dokuritsu Chutai* (white), the No. 2 *Chutai* became the 76th *Dokuritsu Chutai* (red) and the No. 3 *Chutai* became the 74th *Dokuritsu Chutai* (yellow). Due to their common heritage all of these units used an S-shaped flowing tail insignia depicting the river Onga (遠賀川) in Fukuoka Province, Kyushu, which was near their original base at Tachiarai. These units all retained their aircraft in the original Mitsubishi grey-green without use of camouflage.

The 70th *Dokuritsu Chutai*

After being made independent from a parent *sentai*, this unit operated in Manchuria, Taiwan, French Indochina, Thailand, Burma, and then New Guinea. In early 1943 it became active over the north of Australia and later Western New Guinea. In September 1943 it moved to Hollandia and Rabaul from where it operated as the primary headquarters reconnaissance unit for both the 3rd *Hikodan* and its parent the 7th *Hikoshidan*. The unit operated the Ki-46 and also the Ki-51 for shorter-range missions.

The 74th *Dokuritsu Chutai*

This unit re-equipped from the Ki-36 to the Ki-46 in May 1943 before moving to Hollandia the following month. It operated a detachment from But 'drome in July 1943, but after spending less than a year in New Guinea it returned to Japan in March 1944. Because of this timing the unit narrowly avoided the invasion of Hollandia and was then moved to Sumatra in June 1944. It used yellow for its unit colour throughout its New Guinea deployment.

76th *Dokuritsu Chutai*

This unit operated the Ki-46 in Manchuria, Taiwan and the Philippines before advancing to New Guinea where it served the Kyodo *Hikodan* for reconnaissance duty. It was amalgamated into the 10th *Sentai* when this unit was resurrected in June 1943 (see below).

The 76th *Dokuritsu Chutai* was the first JAAF air unit to arrive in New Guinea and had been sent ahead to survey the theatre and thus better inform JAAF commanders of deployment strategies. It arrived in Rabaul on 12 October 1942 from the Philippines, bringing with it ten Ki-46-II twin-engine reconnaissance aircraft as deck cargo aboard the seaplane tender *Sanuki Maru*. About a month later an IJN-IJA inaugural agreement was ratified in respect to air operations in New Guinea, New Britain and the Solomons, committing the 6th *Hikoshidan* to the Southeast theatre. Not quite two weeks later, on 25 October 1942, the 76th *Dokuritsu Chutai* and the JAAF suffered its first loss in the new theatre when Captain Kirita Hideo was shot down by anti-aircraft fire while making a low pass over Henderson Field on Guadalcanal (see Profile 68). Frequently using Gasmata as a forward base, on 19 June 1943 the unit was replaced by the 81st *Dokuritsu Chutai* which had arrived in the theater from Wenchung, Manchuria. The 76th *Dokuritsu Chutai* was then disbanded.

81st *Dokuritsu Chutai*

This unit (not to be confused with the 81st *Sentai*, below) was originally a *chutai* in the 28th *Sentai* activated in June 1939 in Manchuria. In July 1941 it was re-organised as the 28th *Dokuritsu Hikotai*, with three subordinate independent *chutai*, one of which was the 81st *Dokuritsu Chutai*. This unit was deployed to Alexishafen South on 19 June 1943, replacing the 76th *Dokuritsu Chutai*. On 17 January 1944 it returned to Anshan, Manchuria.

Photos of 81st *Dokuritsu Chutai* aircraft are rare. Most evidence of markings comes from wreckage at Hollandia surveyed in April 1944. The unit used a red stripe close to the leading edge of the fin and similarly painted the forward half of the tailplane.

83rd *Dokuritsu Chutai*

Formed in 1939, the 83rd *Dokuritsu Chutai* converted to Ki-51s in February 1941. Initially deployed to Rabaul, the unit soon found itself operating in the Wewak / Madang area, with its main base at Alexishafen North. The unit also conducted a liaison role, its most important VIP passenger being the commander of the 18th Army, General Adachi Hatazo, who was flown from Madang to Salamaua on 2 August 1943. His Ki-51 was escorted by nine 24th *Sentai* Ki-

RECONNAISSANCE UNITS

The tail of Profile 71. This Ki-46-II was sent to Rabaul as a last-minute replacement, transferred from another reconnaissance unit which has yet to be positively identified.

An abandoned 76th Dokuritsu Chutai Ki-46-II at Gasmata which was commonly used as a forward operating base by this unit.

This Ki-51 from an unknown reconnaissance unit captured at Hollandia unusually carries a command stripe across the fin, likely indicating that the aircraft was assigned to the unit commander.

43-II fighters led by the regimental commander Lieutenant Colonel Hachio Yokoyama. The formation was intercepted by US fighters however and Adachi's pilot skirted the mountainous littoral until it was safe to cross Vitiaz Straight at low level. Once there he headed for the cover of New Britain's mountains, and thence Cape Gloucester. The next day Adachi was flown back across the Vitiaz Strait to Salamaua where he praised the troops of his 51st Division. The following month Adachi issued a citation to the squadron, declaring *inter alia*,

> ... its heroic deeds inspired the morale of the ground forces ... their distinguished service rendered great assistance to Army operations ... It is deeply regrettable that the majority of their personnel were either killed or wounded during these operations.

The unit's inventory was all but destroyed by the end of March 1944 by Allied bombing raids and the unit was officially disbanded, along with many other New Guinea units, on 25 July 1944.

A contest was held in early 1942 among the 83rd *Dokuritsu Chutai*'s cadre to choose a unit insignia and the winning design was put forward by pilot Okabe Shoji. The design is a blend of the English number 8 and the *kanji* for 3 (三). Photos in the unit's official history *Gunteibutai no Sokuseki* (Following the Path of an Army Reconnaissance Unit), show the insignia only in white. Many colourful illustrations over the years offer a multiplicity of colours, apparently limited only by the artist's imagination, however these diagrams have no basis in fact.

No. 1 and 2 *Chutai*, 81st *Sentai*

These two *chutai* were equipped with the Ki-46 and mostly undertook liaison and reconnaissance duties. The No. 1 *Chutai* was deployed to Rabaul on 15 April 1943 from Rangoon and operated widely throughout the region from Manila down throughout New Guinea. It also operated at least one Ki-21-I for transport purposes (see Profile 89). Alongside the 76th *Dokuritsu Chutai*, the No. 1 *Chutai* was amalgamated into the 10th *Sentai* in June 1943, becoming that unit's No. 2 *Chutai*, and changing its unit colour from white to blue.

The unit motif is a liberal interpretation of the *kanji* character for one (一) and a triangulated rendition of the English numeral 8. *Chutai* colours were white, red and yellow for the Nos. 1, 2 and 3 *Chutai*. This insignia was also chosen from a competition held among the unit's personnel.

10th *Sentai*

In June 1943 the 10th *Sentai* was reactivated via amalgamating the 76th *Dokuritsu Chutai* and the No. 1 *Chutai* of the 81st *Sentai*. The new unit was commanded by Lieutenant Colonel Shinomura (first name unknown). The No. 1 *Chutai* was led by Captain Shinohara (first name unknown) and retained its red insignia. It moved the bulk of its operations to Alexishafen and Wewak Central in October 1943 but kept a contingent at Rabaul. When the No. 1 *Chutai* of the 81st *Sentai* was incorporated it became the No. 2 *Chutai* and changed its colour to blue. Its *chutaicho* was Captain Nakamura (first name unknown).

The recreated *sentai* answered directly to the 14th *Hikodan* which in turn answered directly to the 8th Army Group. From when it was reformed until it left Hollandia in April 1944, it lost six Ki-46s during missions (both combat and weather-related) and a dozen to Allied air raids. The officer pilots leading the unit were experienced, with an average of 600 flying hours each, as were the Warrant Officer pilots who had around 1,000 hours each. Most of the unit's aircraft evacuated from Hollandia in early April 1944 to Davao in the Philippines, and in mid-1944 the unit returned to Japan to re-equip.

However, in early March 1944, three 10th *Sentai* Ki-46s were deployed to Lakunai to cover the Japanese attacks on the Torokina perimeter in Bougainville. One was shot down by jumpy anti-aircraft gunners over Lakunai as it let down in the circuit area, becoming one of the few "friendly fire" JAAF losses in the theatre. This aircraft was replaced by another Ki-46 sent from Truk. The Torokina patrols were carried out at high altitudes where no enemy threat was encountered, and normally lasted about four hours. These patrols continued throughout the month when an increased Allied air presence over Rabaul shut down the operation.

On 16 March 1944 one Ki-46 was shot down in marginal visibility by 13th Air Force Lightnings near the volcano Tavurvur, just after take-off. The Ki-46 ran into the Lightnings at the same height as it was weaving between showers. Both JAAF crew were killed. On 20 March another Ki-46 was damaged in a taxiing accident at Lakunai. Dismantled and trucked to Vunakanau for repair, it was destroyed by an Allied bombing at the end of 1944. On 28 March the final remaining aircraft was flown to Hollandia with an extra two pilots aboard in order to ferry two replacement Ki-46s to Lakunai that same day. One of these was later badly damaged when it taxied into a bomb crater at high speed, and Allied bombs destroyed the second.

In May 1944 the unit's final Ki-46 at Rabaul was destroyed by strafing. This left the unit with no operational aircraft at Rabaul until September, by which time the crater-damaged aircraft was repaired. It flew to Truk on 2 October with official documents and returned with medical supplies including the much-needed anti-malarial Atebrin. Several reconnaissance flights of the Admiralties were conducted in November, and again on 1 December 1944 and 6 January 1945. Two more liaison flights to Truk were flown on 5 April and 13 July 1945. In the interim, local mapping flights proceeded in the evenings between 1700 and 1800 hours. These ventured only as far as Wide Bay. Other test and practice flights were made about three times a month, always returning by dusk. These flights comprised the last wartime JAAF activity in the New Guinea theatre.

Several of the unit's Ki-46s were named, two known ones being Aoki (青木 - Japanese laurel or blue tree), and Momozono (桃園, named after Emperor Momozono, the 118th Emperor of Japan). At least one of the replacement Ki-46s had served with a previous unit in Japan, with the original markings left on the tail. No example of a camouflaged Ki-46 was surveyed among the numerous 10th *Sentai* wrecks left behind in New Guinea.

PACIFIC PROFILES

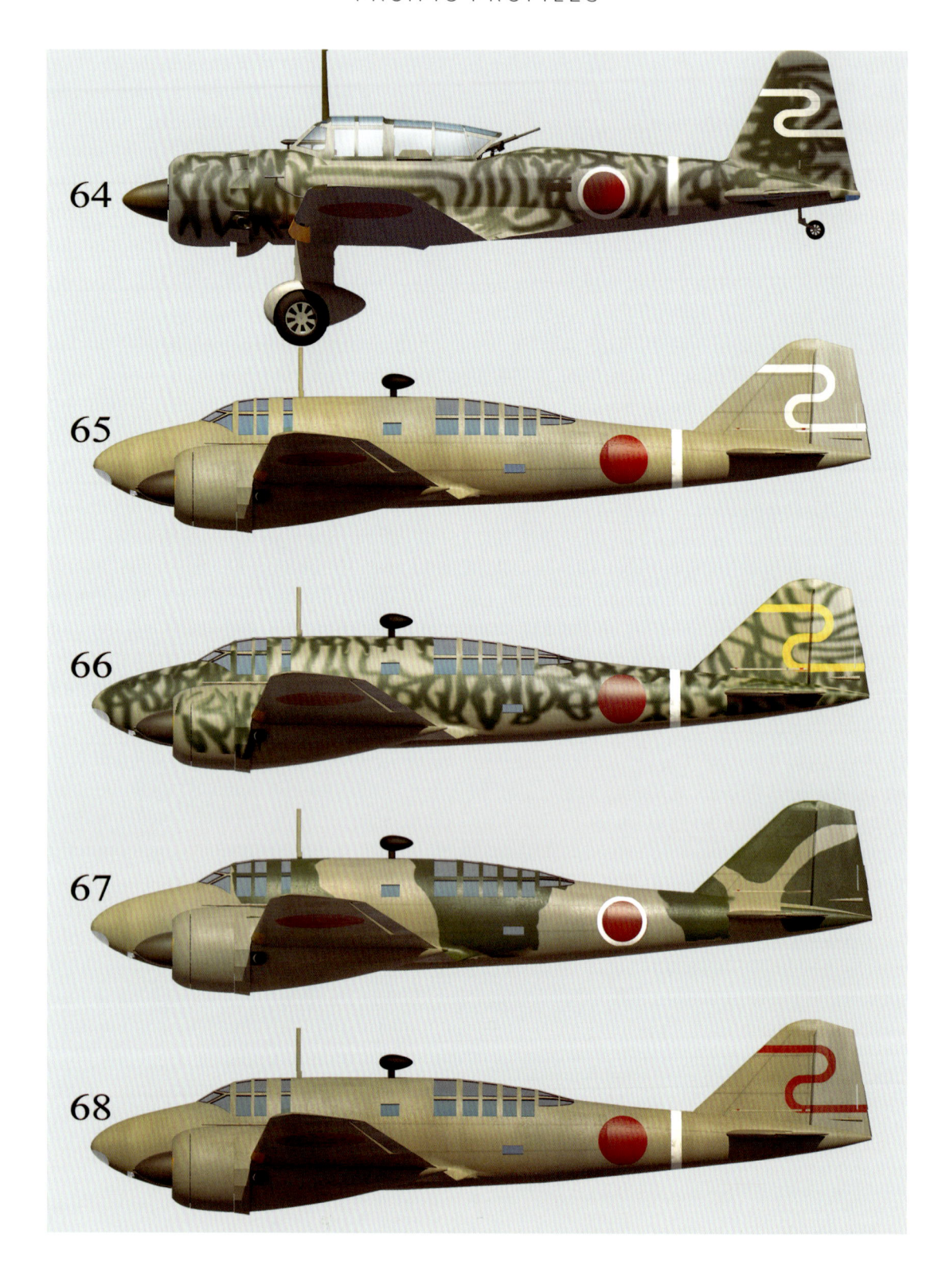

64

65

66

67

68

A diagram showing the timeframe of New Guinea deployments for JAAF reconnaissance units.

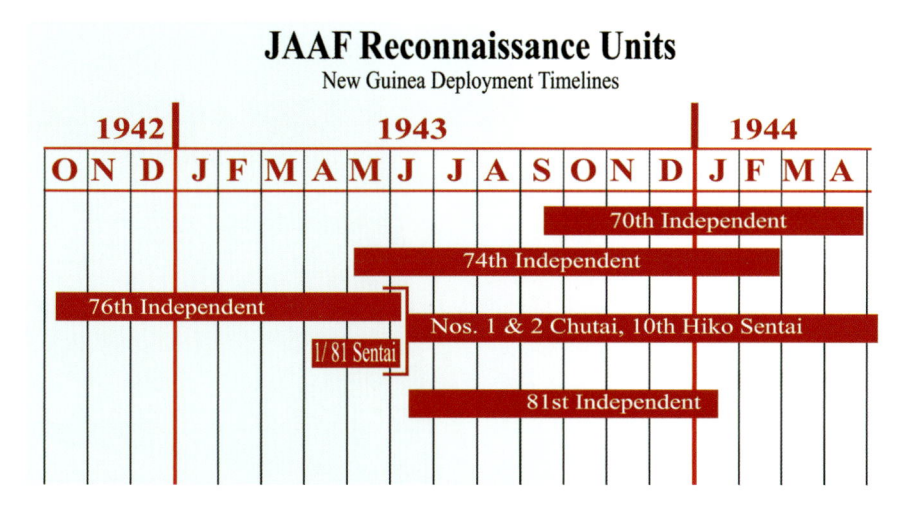

JAAF Reconnaissance Units
New Guinea Deployment Timelines

- 76th Independent
- 1/81 Sentai
- 74th Independent
- 70th Independent
- Nos. 1 & 2 Chutai, 10th Hiko Sentai
- 81st Independent

Profiles 64–68 (Ki-51 Sonia and Ki-46 Dinah)

64. Ki-51 Mitsubishi MN 1240 of the 70th *Dokuritsu Chutai*, abandoned at Hollandia.

65. Ki-46-II Mitsubishi MN 2604 of the 70th *Dokuritsu Chutai*, force-landed near Kimbe, New Britain, on a date unknown in 1943.

66. Ki-46-II Mitsubishi MN 2406 of the 74th *Dokuritsu Chutai*, shot down near But airfield in 1943 on date unknown. Previously assigned to 4th Air Army as illustrated in Profile 50.

67. Ki-46-II 74th *Dokuritsu Chutai*, But airfield October 1943. This airframe had a rare two-tone camouflage scheme.

68. Ki-46-II of the 76th *Dokuritsu Chutai* flown by Captain Kirita Hideo which was shot down near Henderson Field, Guadalcanal, on 25 October 1942.

The subject of Profile 64 at Hollandia. (courtesy Darryl Ford)

PACIFIC PROFILES

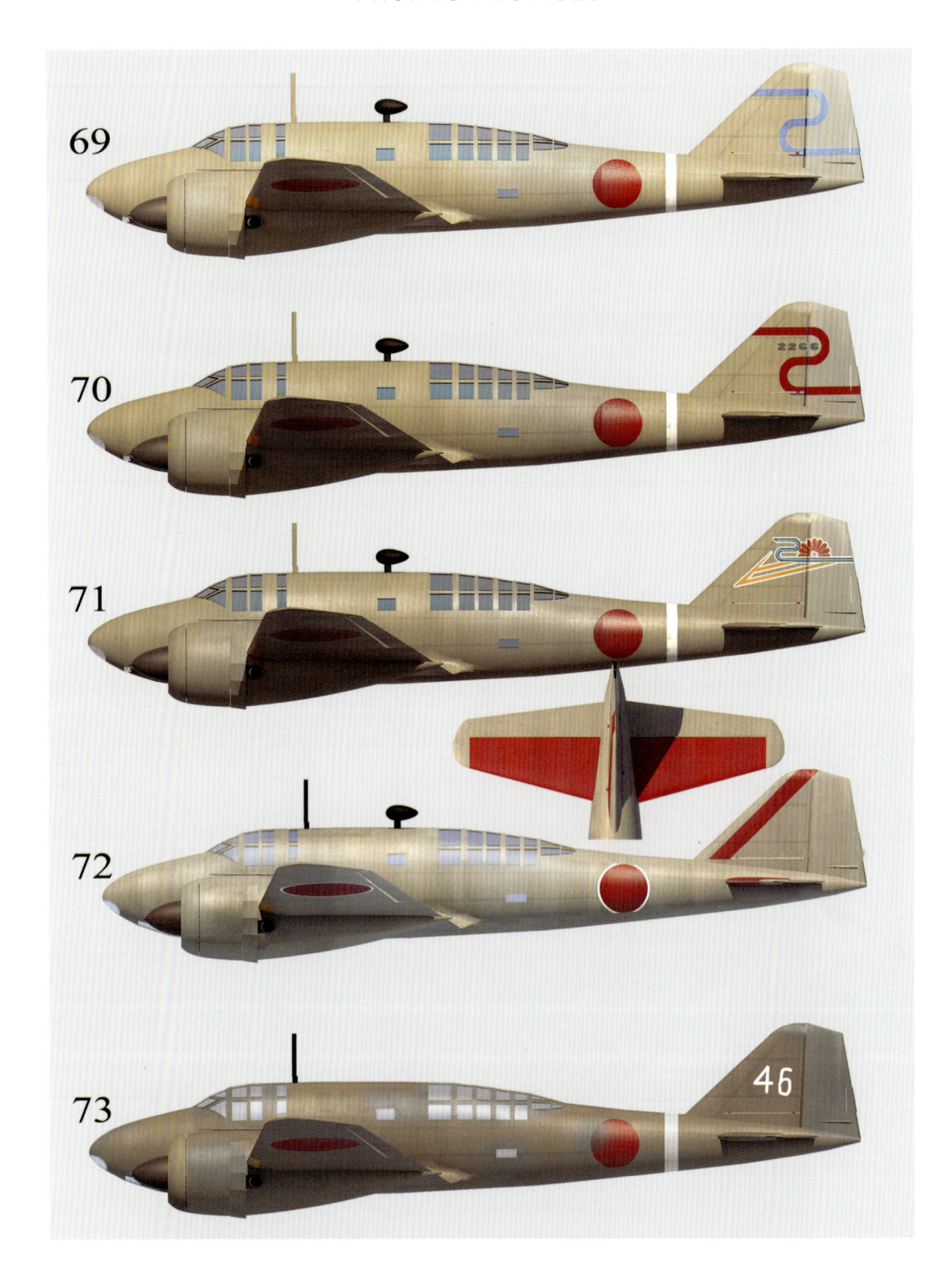

69

70

71

72

73

PAGE 90

Profiles 69-73 (Ki-46 Dinah)

69. Ki-46-II Mitsubishi MN 2049 of the No. 2 *Chutai*, 10th *Sentai*, Wewak 1944.

70. Ki-46-II Mitsubishi MN 2266 of the No. 1 *Chutai*, 10th *Sentai*, captured at Hollandia in April 1944. Note that the MN has also been stencilled on the fin, an atypical practice.

71. Ki-46-II Mitsubishi MN 2783, of the 10th *Sentai*, which was flown from Rabaul to Jacquinot Bay by Captain Iwanaga Norio in September 1945 where it was surrendered to New Zealand forces. This aircraft served previously with an unidentified unit in Japan.

72. Ki-46-II of the 81st *Dokuritsu Chutai* which was abandoned Hollandia in April 1944. Note the red tailplane.

73. Ki-46-II Mitsubishi MN 2846 which was captured at Hollandia and had been assigned to an unknown unit. This aircraft is often profiled as overall blue which is incorrect. There have also been suggestions it was operated by the IJN, however painting all or part of the MN was a unique JAAF practice. The numerals 46 were applied by the Japanese and are not a post-capture marking. This is established by the fact that the marking was noticed long before capture by low-level Allied photography.

The subject of Profile 73. Low-level photography of Hollandia preceding capture established that the numerals were applied by the operating unit.

PACIFIC PROFILES

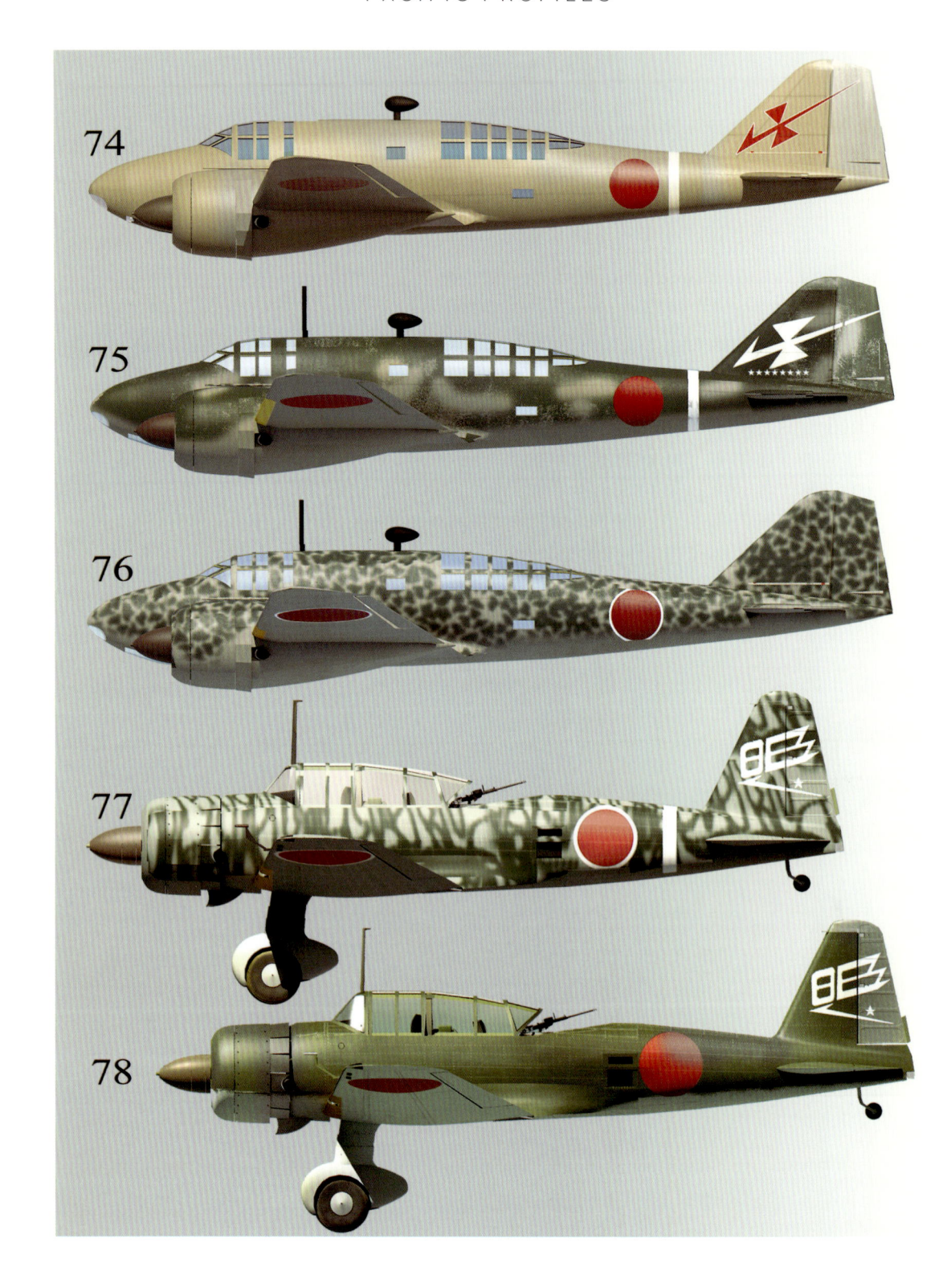

74

75

76

77

78

PAGE 92

Profiles 74-78 (Ki-46 Dinah and Ki-51 Sonia)

74. Ki-46-II Mitsubishi MN 2585 of the No. 2 *Chutai*, 81st *Sentai*, Lakunai in October 1943. Note the thin white piping on the tail insignia.

75. Ki-46-II of the No. 1 *Chutai*, 81st *Sentai*, Lakunai, May 1943. This airframe was one of the few to carry mission markers on the fin.

76. Ki-46-II of the 1st Air Photo Unit which redeployed from Manchuria to Vunakanau in 1943. Unfortunately, nothing further is known of this unit which was likely attached to a higher army command.

77. Ki-51 of the 83rd *Dokuritsu Chutai* at Alexishafen in 1943.

78. Ki-51 of the 83rd *Dokuritsu Chutai* at Alexishafen in 1943.

This photo was taken in Burma but showcases the marking of Profile 75 as it appeared briefly at Lakunai sometime in 1943.

A variety of camouflage colours and schemes on display at Hollandia after its capture. Two 20th Independent Transport Flight insignias are clearly visible on a Ki-49-II and a Ki-21-II in the background. (courtesy Darryl Ford)

The tail of Profile 91 at Hollandia after its capture. (courtesy Darryl Ford)

CHAPTER 14
Transport and Liaison Units

A vast array of dedicated transport units performed logistics and liaison duties in New Guinea, operating alongside and in conjunction with the plethora of JAAF units which comprised the 4th Air Army. Information in this section is largely from captured movements log books which provide considerable details pertaining to despatch deliveries throughout the theatre. Commencing in December 1943, delivery destinations included *inter alia* Wewak, But, Madang, Rabaul, Wakde, Hansa Bay, Dagua, Alexishafen and Ambon. Ports of origin range from as far afield as Manila and Tokyo. The log books helpfully include the unit to which each aircraft was assigned, aircraft type, names of the pilot, and (where applicable) the name or call-sign of the aircraft.

Independent Transport Flights

The main transport units to ply cargoes throughout New Guinea were the 7th, 8th, 9th, 11th, 12th, 20th and 101st Independent Transport Flights (*Yuso Hikotai*). Too small to operate at *chutai* size, these fell under the direct command of 4th Air Army Headquarters and operated between two to four aircraft each, with a mixture of Ki-49, Ki-21, MC-20, MC-21, Ki-56 and Ki-57 transports. To facilitate identification, call-signs were hand-painted in *kanji* and were named after prominent individuals or geographic features in Japan such as towns, cities, rivers or mountains. These characters were modest in size, and commonplace locations in which they were applied include the forward fuselage, rudder or upper fin.

Known *kanji* names associated with respective units are the 101st Independent Transport Flight (Murao and Kimuka), the 11th Independent Transport Flight (Kobayashi, Matsubaka, Kawai, Murakami, Nagai and Sugita), the 12th Independent Transport Flight (Kawasaki, Makabe, Mizusugi, Murata, Sato, Tanaka and Terai [all Ki-49s]) and the 20th Independent Transport Flight (Kagi, Oishi and Otowaki [all Ki-49s]). These units were headquartered at various times from mid-1943 at Wewak, Rapopo and Hollandia.

Civilian Airlines

When the China theatre first opened, the resources of the civilian national flag carrier, Japan Air Transport, were increasingly called upon to move troops and materiel. In December 1938 the Tojo military government created a national monopoly airline through acquisition of a half shareholding in Japan Air Transport. The airline was renamed *Dai Nippon Koku* KK (大日本航空株式会社) and it ran regular services throughout the occupied territories including Korea, Taiwan and Karafuto. In order to reach the distant Pacific Mandates, it used converted Kawanishi H6K4 flying boats. Then, just after the commencement of the Pacific War, the airline was again divided into two separate entities under the control of the IJN and IJA. By late 1943, the IJA was operating regular air routes from Taiwan through the Philippines, NEI, Singapore,

Thailand, southern China and New Guinea (mainly via Hollandia). Most New Guinea routes were operated by Ki-21s and Ki-57s originating from Manila, and which transited Davao, Galela, Babo, and Kamiri as minor hubs. The Southern Air Corporation (*Nanpo Koku KK* 南方航空株式会社) also ran services into the theatre. Names listed for Japan Aviation's Ki-21-IIs include Kakeda, Kawayama, Okamoto, and Sasaki.

Other Units

The Tachikawa Air Transport Department facilitated deliveries of aircrew and aircraft throughout the theatre, as did bombers from the Army Air Evaluation Section. Eighth Army Headquarters operated a detachment of two Ki-57s, mainly deployed to ferry senior officers and VIPs. Other miscellaneous units which operated aircraft in the theatre included communications and airfield detachments. The 1st Air Route detachment operated one Ki-49 and two Ki-21s, one of which was reserved for the unit commander.

Training

Considerable aircrew training was conducted at Hollandia, however it appears that no specific training units were deployed there. Rather, training aircraft were assigned to the units whose pilots were being trained at the time. Two surprise appearances which turned up when Wewak was captured were a Manshyu Ki-79-*otsu* trainer (see Profile 92) and one Tachikawa Ki-55 advanced trainer.

The tail of Profile 81 at Hollandia. The MN 3592 can just be seen stencilled on both the forward rudder and rear fin in white.

The tail of Profile 80 taken by the author at Awar in 1976. Note the number 2 which appears to the bottom left.

TRANSPORT AND LIAISON UNITS

The tail of Profile 88 at Hollandia.

This photo was taken in the NEI, however it is used to show the rare Manshyu Ki-79-otsu trainer, one of which was captured at Wewak as illustrated in Profile 92.

A Mitsubishi MC-21 of Japan Aviation at a base on the Japanese mainland. Profile 96 illustrates one such transport which operated in New Guinea.

A Ki-57 operated by the 101st Independent Transport Flight at an unknown location, the basis of Profile 84.

TRANSPORT AND LIAISON UNITS

The subject of Profile 82 seen at Hollandia shortly after capture. Surrounding it are numerous Ki-46 wrecks from reconnaissance units.

The subject of Profile 80 captured at Awar. A colour photo of this tail is seen in the photo on page X.

This often-published photo was taken on 25 February 1944 from a 17th Photographic Reconnaissance Squadron B-25 Mitchell named Mitch the Witch which shot down the Ki-21-II. The Ki-21 has been universally but wrongly proclaimed as assigned to the 14th Sentai, but this is not the case as that unit had already left the theatre. Instead, the Ki-21 was serving with an unidentified transport unit and was on its way to Rabaul from Wewak. These detachments often applied no tail markings, especially later in the war.

A Dai Nippon Koku KK MC-20 used as an ambulance late in the war. This photo was taken outside New Guinea but exemplifies the combat markings used by this front-line airline.

Taken at Hollandia in early 1944 the mottled camouflage as applied to many Ki-56 transports is exemplified in this staged photo.

PACIFIC PROFILES

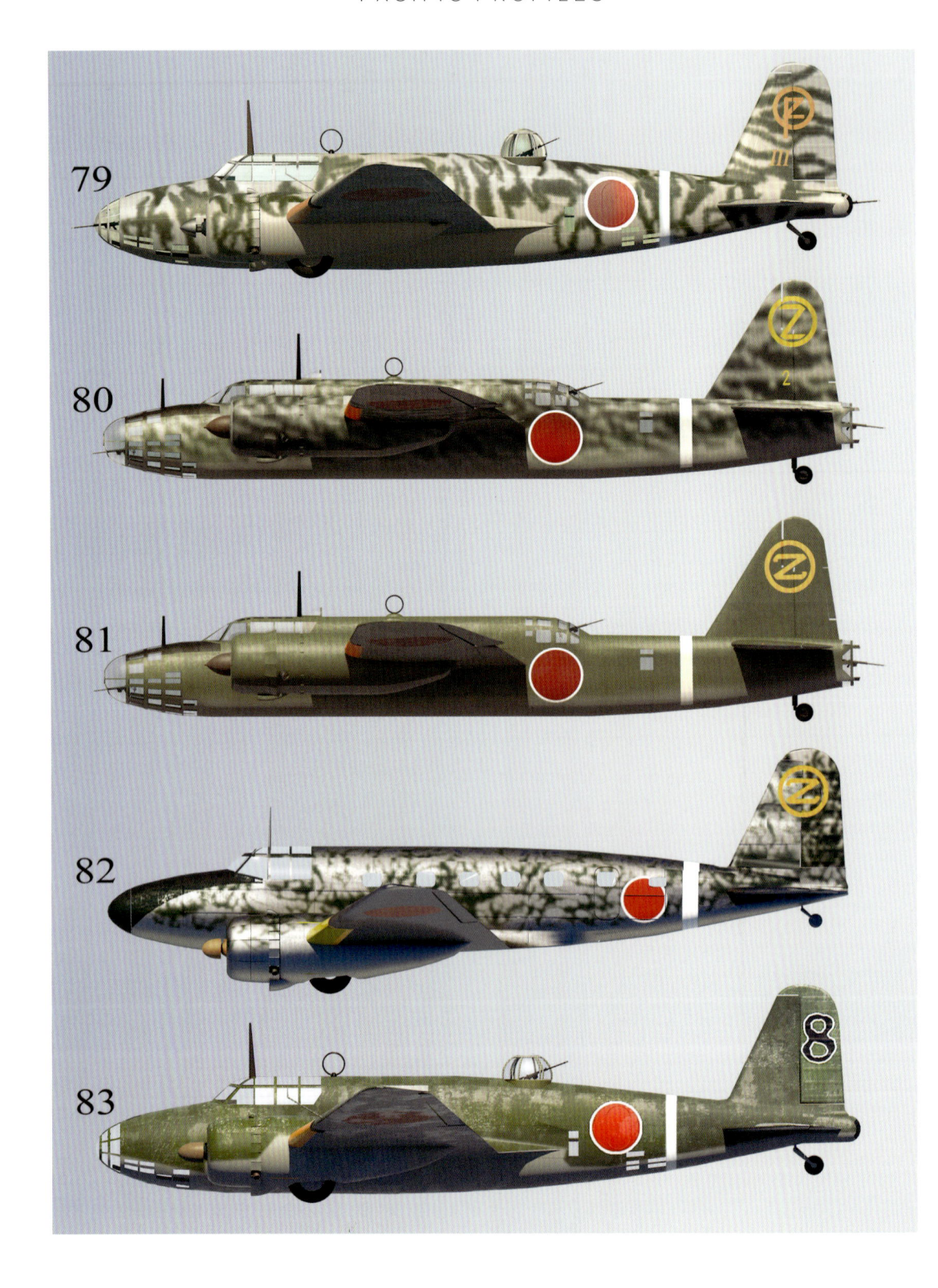

79

80

81

82

83

Profiles 79-83

79. Ki-21-II of the 20th Independent Transport Flight, abandoned at Hollandia. The unit's insignia was a circle with a stylised version of the English numeral 2, painted to appear like the letter "Z". All insignias were hand-painted in yellow.

80. Ki-49-II MN 3342 #2 of the 20th Independent Transport Flight, found at Awar airfield (Hansa Bay). This transport *Donryu* was abandoned after damage incurred from Allied attacks.

81. Ki-49-II MN 3592 of the 20th Independent Transport Flight, abandoned at Hollandia.

82. Mitsubishi Ki-57 MN 1102 of the 20th Independent Transport Flight, abandoned at Hollandia.

83. Ki-21-II of the 8th Independent Transport Flight, at Hollandia in February 1944.

This Ki-21-II is the subject of Profile 79 and is from the 20th Independent Transport Flight at Hollandia. It is unclear why there is a vertical line through the tail insignia.

PACIFIC PROFILES

84

85

86

87

88

PAGE 104

Profiles 84–88

84. Mitsubishi Ki-57 "Murao" 村尾 of the 101st Independent Transport Flight at Hollandia.
85. Mitsubishi Ki-21-II of the 101st Independent Transport Flight at Hollandia.
86. Ki-21-II of the 7th Independent Transport Flight at Rapopo in late 1943.
87. Ki-21-II of the 7th Independent Transport Flight at Rapopo in early 1944.
88. Ki-49-II of an unknown transport unit, found abandoned Hollandia. The two *katakana* characters are ユソ "Yuso" which translates as "transport".

The subject of Profile 85 as captured at Kamiri.

PACIFIC PROFILES

89

90

91

92

93

PAGE 106

Profiles 89-93

89. Ki-21-I of the No. 1 *Chutai*, 81st *Sentai*, at Lakunai, Rabaul, in October 1943.

90. Ki-56 air ambulance, assigned to an unknown unit and abandoned at Hollandia in April 1944.

91. Ki-56 transport assigned to an unknown unit and abandoned at Hollandia in April 1944.

92. Manshyu Ki-79-*otsu* trainer MN 5538 found abandoned at Wewak.

93. Ki-46-II "*Yo*" (ヨ) of an unidentified maintenance unit at Vunakanau, 24 October 1943.

A Ki-56 ambulance at Hollandia, the subject of Profile 90.

PACIFIC PROFILES

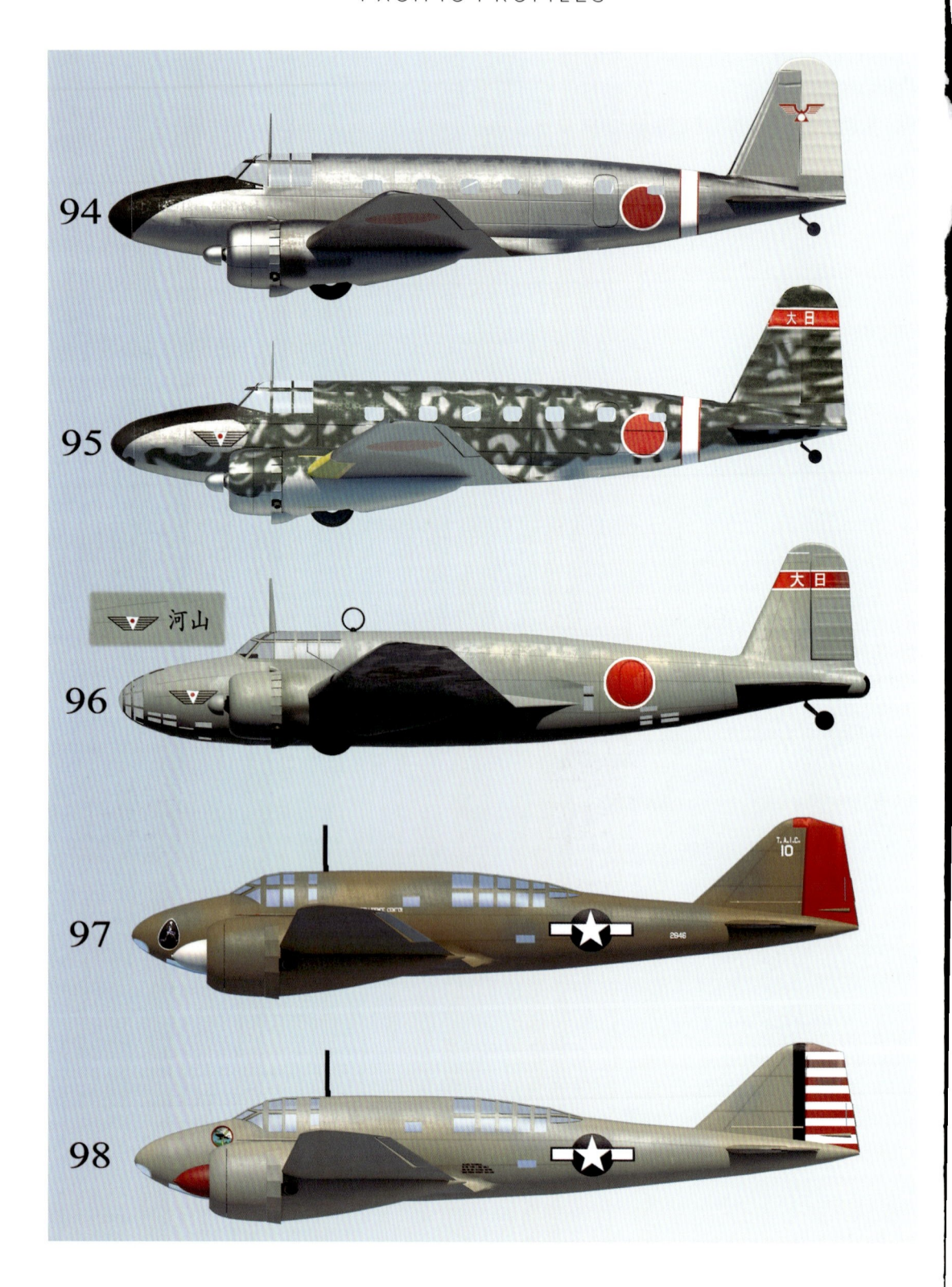

94

95

96

97

98

Profiles 94-98

94. Mitsubishi Ki-57 of the Tachikawa Air Transport Department at Hollandia.

95. Mitsubishi Ki-57 of Japan Aviation at Hollandia in January 1944. The two *kanji* characters within the band on the fin 大 日 *dai ni* are an abbreviation for Greater Nippon.

96. Mitsubishi MC-21 of Japan Aviation named "Kawayama" (河山) at Hollandia in January 1944.

97. Ki-46-II MN 2846 rebuilt by engineers from the 3rd Bombardment Group at Hollandia (also subject of Profile 73). The motif on the nose is "Oscar" the Grim Reaper, which was the 3rd Bombardment Group's adopted mascot.

98. Ki-46-II rebuilt by engineers from the 89th Bombardment Squadron at Hollandia. The circular motif on the nose is the squadron's official insignia.

The Ki-46-II which is subject of Profile 97, seen in the US after its return there for intelligence analysis purposes.

SOURCES

Research focuses on primary sources, including photos (both B&W and colour), intelligence reports, Japanese language sources, post-war wreck analysis, technical reports and diary extracts. Special acknowledgements go to Pacific War Air Historical Associates (PAWHA) members Ed DeKiep, Osamu Tagaya, Darryl Ford for colour photos, Jim Long and deceased members Jim Lansdale and Luca Ruffato. Thanks also to Justin Taylan and his herculean Pacific wrecks website www.pacificwrecks.com.

Russell Harada in Rabaul deserves much credit for his specialist translation work of the archaic Kanji of the WW2 Japanese military, often hand-written. US historian Rick Dunn has conducted leading-edge research on the JAAF in New Guinea from primary source material, including reassessments of JAAF armament and several unit histories. His work has contributed much towards understanding the deployments and modus operandi of the JAAF 4th Air Force.

Japanese POW sources & Diaries

While Allied interrogations of captured JAAF personnel make curious reading and offer leads, they are not definitive. They include POWs from the 1st Air Route, 1st Mobile Air detachment, 5th Signals Section, 10th Independent *Chutai*, 12th Air Sector detachment, 13th, 20th, 22nd, 25th, 38th, 41st and 51st Airfield Construction Battalions, 39th Anti-aircraft Battalion, and interrogations of pilots and aircrew from 11th *Sentai*, 12th Independent Squadron, 14th *Sentai*, 34th *Sentai*, 68th *Sentai*, 77th *Sentai*, 208th *Sentai*, 2nd Air Sector Operations Unit and 248th *Sentai*.

Japanese Language Sources

Diaries/ memoirs of pilots (various units) Tanaguchi Masayoshi, Shishimoto Hironojo, Harumi Takemori, Shiromoto Nauharu, Yoshida Masa'aki, Muraoka Shinichi, Shimizu Kazuo, Katsuaki Kira, Kimura Toshio, and Hasegawa Tomoari. Memoirs of 61st *Sentai* bomber pilot Lieutenant Nitomi (first name unknown), June 1985, and Katsumi Omori, 61st *Sentai* bomber pilot.

Senshi Sosho Tobu Nyu-Ginia Homen Rikugun Koku Sakusen (JAAF Operations, Eastern New Guinea) Tokyo, Asagumo Shinbunsha, 1967

Senshi Sosho Rikugun Koku no Gunbi to Unyo Daitoa Senso Shusen (Equipment and Operations of the Army Air Forces, Asagumo Shinbunsha, 1976

Radio Tokyo transcripts 1943, early 1944

Maboroshi, aircrew recollections privately published in Tokyo in 1986 by the Rabaul-New Guinea Army Air Units Association

Oishi Masayuki, Rikugun Rabauru Kokutai no Shito (The Desperate struggle of Rabaul's Air Army), Maru 10 No 4 (1957)

Letter from Technician Yamanaka to CO Funayama of 14th Field Air Repair Depot, dated 12 March 1943

Gunteibutai no Sokuseki (Following in the Path of an Army Reconnaissance Unit), Unit history of the 83rd *Dokuritsu Chutai*

Translated sources

ATIS intelligence and technical reports (numerous), *inter alia:* Monograph No. 55, prepared by Demobilization Bureau 1950, Southwest Area Air Operations, Phase 1, Monograph No. 31, Southern Area Air Operations Record (Army), December 1941-August 1945, Other monographs pertaining to Operations of 6th and 7th *Hikodan* 1943, and History of 4th *Kokugun*.

SWPA Intelligence Summary No. 126, and 'Armorers' Manual: Reconnaissance Planes, Fighters and Light Bombers', booklet issued by 8th Air Training Unit. Item 4 ATIS Bulletin 1561

Flight Lieutenant L. Green, RAAF Technical Allied Intelligence Inspector, report of aircraft wrecks in Wewak area, 27 June 1945 addressee RAAF Command, Brisbane

Situation Reports, 12th *Hikodan* Headquarters as of 31 December 1942, ATIS Bulletin No. 1174 (Operations Orders and documents pertaining to 14th Field Air Repair Depot, ATIS Bulletin No. 1194

Training Flying Brigade Operations Order No 8 (ATIS Bulletin No. 1329)

Tabulated Records of Movements pertaining to IJN ship deliveries, *inter alia* delivery by *Akitsu Maru* of Ki-43-Is to Truk, December 1942 delivery of 45th *Sentai Sokei* bombers aboard aircraft transporter *Ryuho*, and *Sanuki Maru* pertaining to Ki-46 deliveries to Rabaul.

Japanese Monograph No. 127, Southeast Area Operations Record, Part IV (List of airfields in use and ordnance and fuel expenditure)

Colour Technicalities

For minutiae such as JAAF stencils, propeller markings *et al*, Donald Thorpe's *JAAF Camouflage and Markings WW2* published in 1968 is still the most detailed and most comprehensive reference. Unsurpassed authority for JAAF colour specifics is Nick Millman who runs the website 'Aviation of Japan'.

Index of Names

Adachi Hatazo, General   18, 21, 84
Bong, Richard   61
Endo Misao, Major   29
Endo Tsutomo, Lieutenant   21
Ezaki, Lieutenant   70
Ford, Darryl   20, 27, 30, 56, 59, 60, 82, 89, 94
Fukuda Shigeo, Lieutenant   30
Gojima, Lieutenant   57
Green, Flight Lieutenant L   7, 38
Hachio Yokoyama, Lieutenant Colonel   86
Imai Hidezo, Lieutenant   70
Ishikawa Masayasu, Major   30
Itahana Gi'ichi, Lieutenant-General   37
Itoda, Lieutenant Colonel   29
Iwanaga Norio, Captain   91
Jushiro Ikejima   61
Kanamori, Corporal   33
Kawakita Shozo, Lieutenant   30
Kirita Hideo, Captain   84, 89
Kono, Captain   57
Lynch, Thomas   61
Masui Yoshiro   43
Matubara Kenjiro, Lieutenant   61
Minami Keizo, Warrant Officer   62
Nakaide, Sergeant   33
Nakamura, Captain   86
Nakayama, Lieutenant   33
Nango Shigeo, Captain   70
Noguchi Shigeyuki   50
Oda Akimitsu, Lieutenant Colonel   69, 70
Ogino Koji, Lieutenant   57
Oiwa Mitsuo, Major   57
Okabe Shoji   86
Okami Kinichi, Captain   43
Ota Katsuhiro, Captain   61
Sakai Kazuo, Lieutenant   61
Saito, Lieutenant   70
Sato, Captain   57
Shinohara, Captain   86
Shinomura, Lieutenant Colonel   86

Sudo Einosuke, Lieutenant-General   13
Suzuki Masanori, Captain   21
Takahashi Kenichi, Major   49
Takano Kunihiko, Captain   37
Takayama, Lieutenant   33
Tanaka Shozo, Major   70
Tanaka Sukeharu, Lieutenant Colonel   43, 44
Tarasawa Toshio, Lieutenant   30, 35
Teramoto Kumaichi, Lieutenant-General   13
Toyo'o Sakura   61
Toyokichi Ohnishi, Major   21
Tsukagoe, Sergeant-Major   70
Ueda, Lieutenant   57
Ugakami, Lieutenant   22
Yagi Takeshi, Lieutenant Colonel   61
Yasuoka Mitsuo, Lieutenant Colonel   49, 55
Yoshida Tateki, Lieutenant   37
Yusada Norito, Lieutenant   29